SOVIET LOCAL AND REPUBLIC ELECTIONS

HOOVER INSTITUTION STUDIES: 10

SOVIET LOCAL AND REPUBLIC ELECTIONS:

A Description of the 1963 Elections in Leningrad Based on Official
Documents, Press Accounts, and Private Interviews

MAX E. MOTE

*The Hoover Institution
on War, Revolution, and Peace
Stanford University
1965*

ACKNOWLEDGEMENTS

This paper is the result of investigations carried on at the University of Leningrad during the school year 1962/63. The writer is grateful to the Inter-University Committee on Travel Grants for sponsoring the year of study in the USSR, and to the RELM Foundation for supporting additional study. Suggestions concerning the manuscript were provided by Professor John S. Reshetar of the University of Washington and by the staff of The Hoover Institution on War, Revolution, and Peace. Although grateful for assistance from many sources, the author is solely responsible for all facts and interpretations.

5

CONTENTS

SOVIET LOCAL AND REPUBLIC ELECTIONS

INTRODUCTION

Soviet elections are quite similar in form to those held in the West. And yet there are great differences which alter their essential character. The differences justify a close scrutiny of what is presented by the Russians as the most democratic electoral system in the world. The following pages offer a detailed chronological description of the local and republic elections held in the USSR during 1963, with particular reference to Leningrad where the author was able to observe the events from beginning to end.

Soviet elections have been treated in varying detail in several works in English. The most important, the monograph by Professor Carson, deals with pre-revolutionary electoral practices and with Soviet elections up to 1955. The reader may also consult the specialized work of Professor Swearer. And several basic texts on the Soviet Union present concise summaries of the general aspects of Soviet elections.[1] The present description adds some new material on administrative organization and procedures as well as information from unpublished sources. Three kinds of sources have been utilized: (1) election statutes and city government documents, (2) items from Leningrad newspapers generally not available outside the USSR, and (3) facts recorded during conversations with election officials. In keeping with the general custom, personal sources are not cited by name; others are fully documented.

Local and republic elections were held on two separate Sundays in March 1963. The Leningrad elections were part of those held throughout the Russian Soviet Federated Socialist Republic (RSFSR) on March 3; the same day eight other Union Republics also held elections:[2] the Ukrainian, Belorussian, Uzbek, Kazakh, Moldavian, Latvian, Tadzhik, and Turkmen SSR's. On March 17 the remaining six republics held elections:[3] the Georgian, Azerbaidzhan, Lithuanian, Kirghiz, Armenian, and Estonian SSR's. In addition to the elections to the local soviets and to the Supreme Soviet of the RSFSR, Leningrad elected a few People's Judges to fill vacancies which had occurred since the preceding elections to these posts. Local elections, up to and including the oblast level, have been held every two years since the death of Stalin. Republic elections, to the soviets of the fifteen constituent republics, have been held every four years in the RSFSR since 1947. In addition, elections to the two soviets of the USSR now usually come every

12

four years. The last all-union elections were held in 1962, and will not be considered here. (See Appendix A for the administrative-territorial units involved.)

This paper covers the steps in the election process one by one as they occur; the time involved is about six or seven weeks, from mid-January until after March 3. This is the period during which the undertaking occupied local government and party officials, the press, and masses of the citizens. The campaign begins when the date for elections is set by the Supreme Soviet in a constituent republic of the USSR. Gradually it gains in intensity, reaches a climax on election day, and quickly fades from attention. Appendix F, based on a directive of the Executive Committee of the Moscow City Soviet, shows a timetable for the entire campaign.

While this paper draws heavily on Leningrad materials, the general features described apply to other parts of the USSR. Procedures for elections as set down in law and administrative directives are more or less uniform; this legal uniformity is rein-forced by standard organizational techniques used by the people of the party who stage the elections, a fact true in both theory[4] and practice.

13

1

ORGANIZATION AND ADMINISTRATION

Every administrative-territorial unit of the USSR elects

its own soviet; every voter casts a ballot for one deputy to his re-

public soviet and one for a deputy to every soviet below it within

the hierarchy administering his own domicile. Immediately below

the republic the oblast is the most common administrative-terri-

torial unit, but other units have approximately the same rank--

autonomous oblasts, krais, national okrugs, autonomous republics,

and finally cities subordinated directly to the soviet of the republic,

such as Leningrad and Moscow.

Before 1962 a single oblast soviet administered both fac-

tories and farms. Under Khrushchev's leadership one set of

administrative organs was established to handle industrial matters

and another the problems of agriculture. The party structure was

similarly divided. The reorganization plan was introduced by

Khrushchev at the November 1962 Plenum of the Central Committee

of the CPSU. By early 1963 it was well underway, and the elections
of that year were the first for candidates to the new parallel system
of soviets.

After Khrushchev's ouster, the Central Committee branded
the reorganization as one of his ill-conceived and futile schemes
for solving production problems with unrealistic organizational
changes. The November 1964 Plenum of the Central Commitee re-
versed the 1962 decision, and by early 1965 the party and administrative-territorial structure of the USSR was essentially as it had been
before 1963. For the sake of accuracy, however, the present paper
and appendices describe the dual system as it existed at the time
of the 1963 elections. The reader need only remember that until
1963 and since 1964 oblasts have had only a single oblast-level
soviet.[1]

Appendices A and D illustrate the dual structure. Most
oblasts had two soviets, one industrial and one agricultural. Under
the oblasts the raions, which existed before the reorganization,
were either industrial or agricultural, if the oblast was divided.
Industrial raions were naturally subordinated to the industrial soviet
of the oblast and agricultural raions to the agricultural soviet. The
reorganization did not affect the city of Leningrad directly, since

it is an industrial area.

If the administrative-territorial unit is a krai rather than an oblast, it may have within it a national okrug. Krasnoiarsk krai, for example, has an autonomous oblast and two national okrugs. [2] National okrugs were divided into industrial and agricultural raions just as an oblast was. A national okrug is a permanent administrative-territorial unit with its own soviet formed out of deference to an ethnic group, as the name implies. It must not be confused with the district (also called an okrug) which is created for election purposes only. [3]

Within the industrial and agricultural raions are a variety of lesser administrative-territorial units, such as the village, workers' settlement, settlement, and city. Each of these units usually has its own soviet. [4] Every voter in the USSR thus votes directly for three, four, or five candidates in local and republic elections. The voter who lives in a village votes for deputies to the village, agricultural raion, agricultural oblast (in 1963) and republic soviets. Similarly the voter who lives in an industrial community votes for deputies to the workers' settlement, industrial raion, industrial oblast (in 1963), and republic soviets. Residents of a krai elect the largest number of deputies: one each to the soviets

17

of the village or the workers' settlement, the industrial or agricul-

tural raions, the national okrug, the krai, and the Supreme Soviet

of the RSFSR.

Another atypical situation exists in Leningrad and Moscow,

cities subordinated directly to the republic. There is no intervening

administrative unit between these two cities and the government of

the RSFSR.[5] This means that a citizen of Leningrad proper votes

for three candidates in the local and republic elections (see Appen-

dices B and D), i.e., for a deputy to his city-raion Soviet, one to

the Leningrad City Soviet, and one to the Supreme Soviet of the

RSFSR. A voter living outside the fourteen city-raions of Leningrad

proper but in one of the five raions of Greater Leningrad will vote

for four rather than three deputies. Supposing he lives in the

workers' settlement of Ust'-Izhora, he votes for one deputy to the

Ust'-Izhora Workers' Settlement Soviet, one to the Kolpinskii Raion

Soviet, one to the Leningrad City Soviet, and finally, one to the

Supreme Soviet of the RSFSR.

All-union elections occur every four years, not simultane-

ously with the local and republic elections, and in these elections

every voter casts a ballot for two more deputies, one each to the

two houses of the Supreme Soviet of the USSR.[6] Taking all elections

into account, we find that every voter in the USSR is represented
by a total of five, six, or seven deputies, depending on the kind of
administrative-territorial unit in which he lives.

The election process gets underway when the Supreme
Soviet of a constituent republic announces the date for elections.[7]
The Election Statute requires that lists of election districts be published one and a half months before election day;[8] this would have
been January 16, 1963, and in fact the lists of districts were published in the local papers on January 12.[9]

A district is represented by one deputy; its size depends on
population norms, varying for every level of soviet, and is fixed
by the statute. Because the elections are being held simultaneously
for several levels of soviets, any one point on the map lies in several
different districts for the different soviets. Appendix C demonstrates
this for districts in Leningrad. An immense number of districts were
required for the Leningrad elections; there were 5,746 candidates
and thus 5,746 districts formed.[10]

Responsibility for forming these districts lies with the
executive body of the soviet concerned (with the Presidium of the
Supreme Soviet of the RSFSR, and with the Executive Committees
of lower level soviets). Because size depends on population, detailed

information is necessary. This is supplied by the Housing Boards of the Executive Committees, which in turn get their information from the housing offices scattered throughout the city. One housing office usually administers several apartment houses, and it keeps an accurate running account of the number of citizens living within the area of its responsibility. Every person in the city is listed in the records of some office, and so they are an important, primary link not only in the conduct of elections, but also in the general administration of a Soviet city.[11]

The Soviet term for precinct refers both to the area in which a number of registered citizens vote and the polling places at which they cast their ballots. The area of a precinct is not coterminous with that of a district.[12] In local elections, where thousands of districts are necessary, one precinct is set up for several districts; for example, in Leningrad there were 5,746 districts in 1963 but only 1,637 precincts.[13]

An important factor in the election process is the agitpunkt, literally "agitation point," usually a small office which is headquarters for organizing the propaganda activities of party personnel and volunteers during the campaign. They are not mentioned in the election statute, and their life is generally short; they proliferate

20

during the campaign and disappear soon after. Many functions are carried on from or at the agitpunkt, such as checking lists of voters, meetings with voters, dissemination of literature, and lectures on the Soviet system of government and on economic organization and planning. For example, Leninskii city-raion had set up thirty-five agitpunkts by the time the campaign was launched in January,[14] approximately one office for every seven candidates to the Leninskii City-raion Soviet.

A permanent establishment for disseminating propaganda is the "red corner, " a room or a corner of a factory, apartment, institution or other organization, where propaganda placards, charts, and literature are usually on display. These are sometimes converted into agitpunkts for the few weeks of the election campaign.

The next stage of the process is the selection of election commissions. There are three separate types of commissions: for administrative-territorial units such as a republic or city, for districts within administrative-territorial units, and for precincts. A Central Election Commission for the RSFSR prescribes the forms for ballots and the general procedures for subordinate district and precinct commissions.[15] Announcement of the event is one of the early signs of the coming election campaign.[16]

The main function of the district commission is merely
to register the selected candidate; since there is one candidate
per district, each district commission registers one person. Some
of its other functions are to: supply polling places with ballots,
determine the results of elections for its own district, supply the
elected deputy with a certificate of election, and submit its records
to the corresponding Executive Committee for deposit.[17] Commissions for RSFSR districts perform essentially the same functions as those for the lower level districts of local elections.[18]
With one commission for every district and thus for every candidate,
it is clear that in a country which in 1961 elected 1,822,049 deputies to local soviets,[19] the official side of the elections is in itself
a mass undertaking.

Precinct commissions operate the polls on election day
and count the ballots. Besides this they correct the lists of voters,
submit a report on the voting, and submit their records to the
appropriate Executive Committee.[20]

The total of 56,365 persons serving on election commissions of all three types in the city of Leningrad (see Appendix H)
includes only those who are official commission members. Many
more people serve as voluntary propaganda workers.

2

PRELIMINARY PROCEDURES

Elections are run off practically without contest, and the actual "electing" is completed long before people go to the polls. In 1961 a total of 1,821,000 deputies were elected, while only 249 of those nominated failed to get a majority of votes.[1] This means that when nominated a candidate has one chance in almost ten thousand of not being elected. So it is clear that the choice of candidates is not made on election day. Nor is it made at the official, public nomination meetings. These too are run off in a predetermined, pro forma style without contest or incident. Candidates are actually "elected" in small, closed meetings at the very outset of the whole campaign.

Selection of Candidates

The selection of candidates begins about the time the newspapers are giving their first indication of the coming campaign, the announcement that election commissions are being formed. The first commission has to be formed forty days prior to election day; this was January 20, 1963, and in mid-January organizations begin to check their rosters for eligible persons. The candidates have to be selected and registered twenty days prior to the election, so there is a period of some three weeks, between the fortieth and twentieth days before election time, in which the various organizations begin the task of actually selecting the people who will run.[2]

Only organizations have the right to advance candidates for the office of deputy, which means that the selection is also a matter for the organizations to perform. The statute on local elections gives the right of nomination to party and social organizations, unions, cooperatives (e. g. kolkhozes), youth organizations, and cultural societies. Corresponding stipulations exist for both local and republic elections.[3] For a fairly typical experience, we will look at the nomination procedure in a factory. Most meetings are held at the place of employment, for it is here that personnel records are on file with information about a worker's labor record; it is here that candidates are known to large numbers of easily assembled people.

The smallest organizational unit of a typical factory is the brigade of workers headed by a brigadier and consisting usually of less than a score of persons; a few brigades make up a shop, and a collection of shops constitute a factory. In some cases two or more factories may be joined in an industrial complex known as a kombinat. Parallel to this framework, the factory or kombinat supports two other organizational structures, one for the party apparatus and one for the union. The principal unit for the former is the party committee, and for the latter a union committee. These are small groups which have first-hand information about personnel, and they begin the process of selecting candidates.

In order to see how union officials select a candidate in close cooperation with the factory party-organization, a conversation on this topic is reconstructed. This is a real conversation in the sense that all the questions and answers have been transcribed from conversations with members of the factory, union, and party units engaged in the business of selecting candidates. It is artificial only in the sense that the conversation has been rearranged to secure continuity. Let us now assume that we are in a Soviet factory, talking to union and party organizers, asking them questions about the nomination procedure.

Q: Precisely who is it that nominates the candidates?

A: Organizations nominate them. The election statutes require this.

Q: Would it be possible for a group of citizens, say the people who live in one neighborhood, to get together and decide to send "their" candidate to the local soviet, perhaps with a specific legislative assignment to carry out on their behalf, once the candidate is installed as deputy?

A: No, this doesn't happen. An individual worker may get up in a meeting and recommend someone for candidacy, but this takes place in the meeting of some organization. People don't form groups for the purpose of nominating a man. Such a group would not be a registered organization, and therefore it would not have the right, according to law, to nominate anyone. I understand what you are thinking about, but this kind of thing does not occur in the Soviet Union.

Q: Within the organization, then, who chooses the man who will be nominated later on?

A: This is done by the party or union committee in the factory. The fact is that the party and union work closely on this.

Q: How do the committees do it--is there some kind of a meeting of the union or party members, called for the purpose of selecting a man for candidacy?

A: There is a series of meetings. The first one is attended by a small number of people, and they go over the personnel files of the workers. Then there is another meeting, and more people are present. The number of persons attending the meetings grows as the process continues.

Q: Then by the time an open assembly nominates the candidate, there have been several meetings of the party and union groups to decide on who the candidate will be?

A: That is correct.

Q: When do these preliminary meetings begin?

A: They begin about the time the announcements of elections begin to appear in the newspapers.

Q: Sometime in January, if I am not mistaken?

A: Along in January.

Q: What kind of man is it that the selection committee chooses?

A: The best man. After all, we know the man's biography and have studied his characteristics. We don't choose someone who has just come to work for us.

Q: But what if you are mistaken in your choice?

A: We are seldom mistaken. Of course, it can happen that deep inside a man's character are traits which are difficult to see from his biography and which come to light only after the man is in office. But if such a thing happens, let's say a man drinks or steals, we can recall him. There is a new law on recall and it is easier to remove a man from office than it used to be. [4]

Q: Well, then, what happens if you choose a man for candidacy and the voters don't like him--will they reject the candidate on election day?

A: This happens very rarely. If a mistake has been made, there is recall.

Q: Exactly what qualities do you look for in a deputy?

A: First of all, a candidate has to have authority. He has to be a good worker. He should work conscientiously and when given a task carry it through to the end. And he should be well known, so that he commands the respect of people. We like people with experience in organizational work, people who have spent time doing things for others. This is the kind of a person who will make a good deputy.

Q: How many candidates do you select?

A: We select one candidate for every opening. For example, in our city-raion there are 250 deputies to the city-raion soviet, so this means there will be 250 candidates.

Q: Doesn't it sometimes happen that you choose two candidates for one office?

A: I have heard that this sometimes happens out in the villages, but I have never seen it. You see, it would indicate a lack of confidence in the candidate if you were to nominate two men for the same post. It would mean you think one of them is not good enough for the office. We don't want to insult our candidates.

Q: Who arranges this so that it comes out even--one candidate for every office?

A: This is arranged by the party. It is their job to assign us the required number of candidates. They tell us how many.

Q: Another question in regard to this. Your factory, for example, has some shops located in other places in the city, yet the factory as a whole is nominating just one candidate to the Supreme Soviet of the RSFSR. There are different parts of your factory within election District 97. Isn't it possible that in the other parts of this factory, in other sections of town, the workers there will decide to choose a different candidate? Maybe you will, after all, end up with two candidates from the one district.

A: No, this will not happen. The man we are going to nominate has been settled on in advance, and so we will simultaneously nominate the same man in both parts of the factory.

Q: Who decided on this man?

A: This was decided on in the earlier meetings.

It is quite clear from this that the nomination of candidates is carried out very early in the election process, in small meetings headed by union and party organizers, and that the candidates are chosen on the basis of characteristics recorded in their personnel files and on the basis of the judgment of organizers who have known them for some time. The candidates are respected, natural leaders, and once chosen they have a 10,000 to 1 chance of being elected.

From the Soviet point of view, this is entirely reasonable. As Lenin said, soviets aren't talking shops,[5] and candidates are chosen to carry out orders. They are not there for the purpose of carrying popular demands to a parliamentary assembly. So efficient organization is needed, especially when one considers the huge number of candidates to be decided upon in a large area like Leningrad with its 5,746 deputies chosen in a single election. The selection of candidates could not be left to chance or to spontaneous forces. To call this an election in the Western tradition of parliamentary government is absurd; while the formality of creating districts and selecting candidates has been preserved, the political meaning of the act has been carefully eliminated.

In the above conversation, it was stated that only one person is nominated for every district. It often happens that two persons are in fact nominated from the same district. One of the persons usually is a worker from the area, and the other candidate is a member of the Central Committee of the party. Khrushchev was nominated in scores of districts throughout the country, simultaneously with one other candidate. But only in the Kalininskii District of Moscow was Khrushchev the solitary candidate. Similarly Frol Kozlov was nominated in more than one district of the RSFSR, but only in District 90 of Leningrad was he the solitary candidate. But the Central Committee of the CPSU later published an open letter, assigning its members to the districts from which they would in fact run for the Supreme Soviet. Central Committee members were of course assigned to the districts where they had been the solitary candidates, and this in effect withdrew their nomination from all other districts where workers had nominated them along with a local person.[6] It is clear that even this slight variation on the standard practice, the dual nomination, is not left to chance. To paraphrase a Soviet election official, not only the "best people" get elected-- the right people get elected.

Nominations

The next major step in the campaign, and an important
one because it is open to the public, is the formal nomination of
candidates in meetings of organizations, factories, and other col-
lectives such as kolkhozes. Nominations have a publicity function,
but no meaning as far as the actual selection of candidates is concerned.[7] Large meetings are organized for prominent candidates,
those of the Supreme Soviet of the RSFSR. Small meetings are held
for the introduction of candidates to city-raion and city soviets. The
main difference is that the smaller meetings require less effort
and organizational work, tend to be a bit less formal and ceremonious.

Candidates must be registered twenty days before the
election,[8] which was February 10, 1963; the press began to publish
announcements of nominations on January 29. The first one was for
N. S. Khrushchev and I. D. Leonov in District 84 of Leningrad.[9]
Announcements were in the papers until about February 6, when
most of the RSFSR nominations had been reported. Supreme Soviet
candidates receive favored treatment; almost all of them had individual articles in the local press, whereas few of the city and city-
raion soviet candidates received any individual attention. The city

television studio also tried to devote five or ten minutes to publicizing each Supreme Soviet candidate.

RSFSR nomination assemblies may be used for speeches of major importance. For example, Frol Kozlov came to Leningrad for a few days' visit and spoke to the voters of Moskovskii District 90 at the Gor'kii Palace of Culture on February 26.[10] This was a major political event for the city. On February 27 Nikita Khrushchev likewise appeared in Moscow at a meeting of voters of the Kalininskii District to give a speech of major foreign-policy importance.[11]

Still in the category of large meetings are those conducted for local residents who are candidates to the Supreme Soviet of the RSFSR. A typical nomination meeting of this level may draw as many as five hundred persons to a club or Palace of Culture. The procedure is standardized: After the national anthem, the chairman takes the floor and asks for a motion to approve the presidium of the meeting, whereupon the twenty or twenty-five persons chosen file solemnly to the stage; these people are workers or prominent people in the district itself and are being publicly honored. The next step is the lead-off speech, highly patriotic, filled with data about accomplishments of the government and party and with plans for the immediate and distant future. There is a good chance that in this speech a member of the party's Central Committee will be nominated. Following this comes a series of five or six speeches, each lasting about five minutes. Each one makes two points: the progress of government and party, and the good qualities of the candidate, in that order of presentation and importance. These speeches are flowery, patriotic campaign oratory; they are filled with standard phrases and clichés, and vary only in the quality of elocution. The nominations advanced in these speeches are voted on with a show of hands and are always approved unanimously.

After the candidate is approved, the next step is to vote on a list of "sworn supporters." The rule is that every candidate must have at least one official supporter, who is responsible for agitating for his nominee during the campaign. Supreme Soviet candidates have several of these supporters. A list of their names and addresses is read off, and another unanimous vote approves them. The final gesture is to send an appeal to the candidate to accept the nomination since he is not present at the meeting. Typically this will be a telegram to the Central Committee member, or a letter to the local candidate. An open vote is taken on this step, again mechanical and unanimous. Such a meeting lasts about an hour and a half, and closes with all rising again for the national

34

anthem. It is a solemn civic ceremony. When it is over, some kind of entertainment is offered the audience, perhaps a movie or the favorite of Russian entertainments, an amateur talent concert.

Ritualistic solemnity characterizes the entire affair. It is a state service and the atmosphere is not one to elicit conflicting opinions and pressures; to disturb the ceremony would be in very bad taste. The whole thing takes place in a pro forma manner, devoid of spontaneity, and the attention of the audience may consequently wander. Voting is unanimous, as mentioned, and the air about the auditorium is such that only the most audacious upstart would dare to disturb it. And so the sessions wear on, generally without incident or interest. Those sections of the party apparatus concerned with mass work organize the assemblies, get out the crowds, and provide the people with some reward for coming, in the form of post-meeting entertainment.

The smaller nomination meetings follow the same general pattern, but present more candidates to smaller audiences. These meetings usually occur on the premises of the organization nominating the candidates, usually a factory, institute, or other collective. They may be conducted during the lunch hour or right after work and last perhaps half an hour.

The procedure parallels the one described above. First the chairman, usually the head of the institution's union committee, calls the gathering to order and takes the vote for the presidium of the meeting. The members of the presidium take their places on the podium. Supporting speeches for the candidates begin. Perhaps three to six candidates will be nominated to the city-raion and city soviets. The speeches have to be short and they follow a pattern containing the following elements, all of which the speaker has to get across in three or four minutes: (a) the initial assurance that the candidate is a superlative worker, (b) a short biographical sketch of the candidate, giving his class origin and employment background, (c) a statement about the high degree of social con-sciousness of the person, meaning a history of his activity in or-ganizations, and (d) an expression of the conviction that the candidate will justify the trust placed in him (to "justify the faith of the voters" is one of the most common clichés of the election vocabulary). The nominations are approved by an open vote, again unanimous. Then a list of "sworn supporters" is read off and voted on. A candidate to a lower level soviet usually has just one supporter, those to a city soviet a handful. This ends the meeting, a short one which can be fitted into a lunch hour or a brief session after work.

36

The candidates are nominated according to a highly routine procedure, and during the ceremony scarcely a voice is heard from the floor, although the atmosphere is not nearly as formal as at the larger meetings. Conceivably a person might speak up from the floor at these gatherings, but as a rule they are something which a captive audience hurries through and away from. All audience expressions are unanimous ("unanimously" is another much-used word at election time).

After attending several of these meetings, certain specific questions about the procedure remained unanswered. Here are some of them, as put to various professional people of the administrative and party system:

Q: At these meetings we observe candidates being
approved for nomination. Statistics show that once
a man is nominated, he is almost certain to be
elected. What I am getting at is that a very small
percentage, therefore, of the voters participate
in the selection of deputies. Take the example
of a Supreme Soviet candidate, who according to
the statute represents 6,000 citizens. Only about
500 people attend the nomination meeting, and the
candidate is approved without objections, without
even any discussion. Or take the city-raion candidate,

where a deputy represents 500 people. The nomination meeting may be attended by some 200 people, again with uncontested results. Now does it ever happen that people rise during these meetings and object to the nomination of a given candidate? Or is the nomination always automatic?

A: Not always. I have heard of cases out in the villages where some people objected to a candidate. But I never heard of it happening in Leningrad.

Q: But what if you don't like the candidate who is suggested?

A: In this case the deputy can be recalled after his election.

Q: Another thing. You nominated four candidates at this meeting. One for each district. How did you know how many to nominate?

A: We got word from above.

Q: What does that mean?

A: From the people in the party apparatus who organize the nominations. They let us know whom to nominate.

Q: What about the candidates who were chosen today-- do they have experience or other qualifications in administration?

A: That is not necessary. We pick good people who have

a sense of responsibility and who will carry out the tasks which are assigned to them.

This raised an interesting point about a deputy's preparation for office, and the following questions were asked of a new candidate prior to the elections:

Q: Have you been studying up on the work of the candidate and the deputy? Have you read any books or pamphlets on your future work in the soviet?

A: No.

Q: How will you know what to do?

A: The old deputies will tell me.

Q: Is that all?

A: No, there will be lectures given by the Executive Committee members, instructing us in our duties.

Q: Then you have no prior experience in the work of a deputy?

A: No, but they'll tell me what to do, and I'll carry out my assignments. But it's too early to worry about this now.

Considering the manner in which candidates are selected, it is obvious that nomination meetings are held primarily for their publicity value. The meetings proceed without debate, questions, or opposition, because the nomination itself has been carried out earlier by members of the party and union committees. At the public nomination, names are in fact presented for inspection to a small proportion of the electorate. The candidates are in reality people of very high caliber in their own line of work, but this does not mean they are equipped with any special knowledge of or interest in the deputy's work as such. They are leading people, commandeered to their public posts because they are the ones most likely to command general respect.

Registration

After the nomination of candidates, the next step is to register them with the district election commissions. For candidates of the Supreme Soviet of the RSFSR, this has to be done twenty days prior to the elections,[12] which was February 10, 1963. According to the newspapers, registration was completed on time, and the final list of candidates appeared in the paper on February 19.[13] The deadline for registration of candidates to the city and city-raion soviets is fifteen days prior to elections (February 15, 1963),[14] and on February 16 the local paper reported that all candidates had been duly registered on time.[15]

40

The procedure for registration is simple: After the nomination meeting, the chairman and the members of the presidium of the meeting submit two documents to the district commission.[16] One is a letter from the candidate recording his willingness to run. An example of such a letter is shown in Appendix J. The other is a protocol of the meeting, certifying that the chosen candidate was selected in accordance with the statute. On the basis of this, the district commission submits a report to the election commission of the corresponding administrative-territorial unit to whose soviet the man will be elected (e. g. to the city or city-raion commission in Leningrad).[17]

All this is supervised by the Executive Committee of the appropriate soviet. From articles in the local papers it appears that this is probably the responsibility of the General Department and the Organization-Instruction Department of the Executive Committee; the latter is mainly responsible for on-the-job training of deputies after they have been installed in office.[18] Both departments work closely with the party organs that handle selection, nomination, and publicizing of candidates. The secretary of the Executive Committee also has a prominent part in all these undertakings.

On the basis of these reports from the district commission,

registration is completed. The city and city-<u>raion</u> election commissions publish their lists of candidates, which have to be made available to the public prior to the elections.[19] These lists bear the name, profession, and party affiliation (i. e. , Communist Party member or not) of the candidates. For RSFSR and city soviet candidates, they are published in the newspapers.[20] For lesser candidates they are displayed in office buildings or on public bulletin boards.

Lists of Voters

About this time, lists of voters are drawn up and corrected.[21] These are typewritten sheets showing the name and address of all voters; their compilation is supervised by the Executive Committee of the lowest level soviet in a given area from information supplied by the housing offices. The lists are made public twenty days prior to the elections and from that day on, right up to election eve, it is the duty of the voter to go by and make sure that he is properly entered on the lists. He receives a slip in the mail reminding him of this and telling him the address of the place he can check the lists, usually a district or precinct commission office or an <u>agitpunkt</u>. The voter presents some document, usually his internal passport, from which the entry on the list is verified. Members of the various commissions supervise the lists as an unpaid public

service; each member serves perhaps two or three evenings during

the course of the election campaign.

People's Judges

In addition to the local and republic elections, there were

in 1963 special concomitant elections in Leningrad to fill the vacant

offices of eight People's Judges in five city-raions. The People's

Judges are elected to the People's Court of each city-raion. All

this is regulated in Leningrad by the Executive Committee of the

Leningrad City Soviet[22] which decreed that elections to fill these

posts would also be held at the same time as the other elections.[23]

The procedure for these elections is spelled out in Chapter

VII of the Statute on the Election of People's Courts, and is some-

what similar to the procedure for electing deputies. Election

districts are formed, along with their commissions, ten days in

advance of the elections, the lists are checked beginning ten days

in advance, the candidates are registered seven days in advance,

and the lists of candidates are made available to the public five days

in advance.[24] Eight judges were elected for five-year terms in

Vasileostrovskii, Kirovskii, Nevskii, Oktiabr'skii, and Smol'ninskii

city-raions.[25]

3

CAMPAIGN AND ELECTION

The final stages of the campaign are, quite naturally,
marked by an intensification of publicity. The statute for local
elections says that the voters must be informed daily of the date
and place of elections during the twenty days prior to the balloting. [1]
Thus we find in the local press even before this date, which was
February 10, 1963, frequent biographies of the candidates. [2] Later,
such articles appeared daily. Ten days before the election, ballots
have to be sent to the polling places by the district commissions. [3]
Polling places are prepared for voting and in well managed areas
are subjected to public inspection. Then, during the last ten days
or so, door-to-door work by the agitators begins; the aim is to
visit every single voter and explain the meaning of the election and
present biographical information on the candidates. Also during the
final stage it is the goal of the party to have every candidate meet
at least once with the voters of his district; these meetings with
voters serve two purposes: they give the candidates and organizers

an opportunity to present the policy of the government to the people, and the candidates an opportunity to learn and record the wishes or instructions of the voters.

In the week or ten days before the election, attention is turned to the achievements of the Soviet regime vis-a-vis the old tsarist regime as well as Western countries. The superiority of the Soviet system and the glory of its achievements are preached day and night, in meetings, in the papers, and on the radio. It was not just a coincidence[4] that right before elections, immense lines could be seen at some of the Leningrad stores and sidewalk stands: Rare and delectable things were being sold. Eggs were back on the market for the first time since the previous fall (at about ten cents each), and oranges seemed suddenly abundant when compared with the winter months (when they sold for about forty cents each--if the stores had them). The Soviet regime at election time is asking for a vote of confidence in the government and its achievements. So the regime apparently feels the necessity of putting tangible evidence of its achievements into the hands of the electorate. And eggs and oranges appear. At the same time, the evils of the bourgeois world and the anti-democratic machinations of Western politicians, especially Americans, are dwelt on with intensity and ferocity.

The Press Campaign and the Ideal Soviet Deputy

The events described hereafter are taking place simultaneously. We begin with the final stages of the press campaign in
which almost entire issues of the local papers are filled with
election items. The newspaper campaign for prominent candidates
to the Supreme Soviet of the RSFSR opens about three or four weeks
prior to election day. Leningrad papers published series of articles
and pictures giving personal biographies of about three-fourths of
the city's twenty-three candidates to the soviet of the republic. The
local Vechernii Leningrad began a series called "Our Candidates"
on February 6, and Leningradskaia Pravda started its articles
headed "Candidates of the People's [or, variously, 'Indestructible']
Bloc" on February 12. Candidates to the city and city-raion Soviets
received almost no individual coverage. Leningradskaia Pravda
carried a picture of a City Soviet candidate on February 22, and
Verchernii Leningrad had articles on city and city-raion candidates
late in the campaign on March 1. [5]

Newspapers publish highly stereotyped campaign literature;
to give a representative example and impart some of the flavor,
the following article is quoted in full: [6]

46

Our Candidates for Deputy:
Everyday Events Deserving Praise

Some biographies seem so simple and ordinary that you
don't know what to say about them at first. Tamara Dmitrievna
Mitrakova feels she has done nothing heroic. She has worked under-
ground many years. No startling episodes, no dazzling promotions...

But if you take a close look at every day which she lives
through, weigh what she does for people, it becomes clear: these
ordinary days, this life deserves praise. Because always and in all
things Tamara Mitrakova was with the people--in sorrow and in joy,
in the days of wartime tribulation and of peacetime labor.

One autumn day in 1941 she went to the Frunzenskii City-
raion Soviet. There they sent her to a repair-train unit.

... The twelve hour shift was coming to a close. The
frozen earth creaked, the rails squeaked as they were being piled
in a stack. But neither the faces nor the hands of the repair workers
felt the deep frost. The cutting wind chafed their skin. Work that
day went slower than usual. They advanced cautiously. Two days
earlier a repair worker had been blown up by a mine laid by the
Fascists under a tie.

Tamara brought up the gravel, thinking that she would not
go to the warming hut. A long way to go, and she was too tired. She
would lie down right there in the snow, like yesterday, and have a
good nap.

Searchlights lit up the thick gloom. The low rumble of a
motor could be heard. Some military person was driving up in a
car. "The Commander of the Front," Tamara heard a loud whisper.
The general approached the workers.

"Comrades," he said loudly so all could hear, "much depends on you now. The breakthrough of the Leningrad blockade has begun. But how can we get troops through if there is no rail line?"

"Work through tonight? No--I can't hold out," sounded in her brain. The general continued to speak. The girl saw him through a shroud...

"Let's give our word. Tonight we'll finish the spur," said the brigadier [of the work crew] laconically and solemnly, as if it were a vow.

The fatigue slipped away somewhere, like a weight rolling off their backs, falling from their hands. Like getting your second wind. Tossing the gravel with her shovel, she looked at her comrades. It was hard for them, but they were holding out. She would not give in either.

That night the repair workers kept the word which they had given to the general.

Somewhat later the train on which Mitrakova served was transferred to the Carpathians.

*   *

Tamara Dmitrievna's form-jumbo and the form men work with well coordinated rhythm. The brigadier gives the signal and the arm of the form-jumbo carefully puts the section of the form into place. The laborers haul off the muck. There is a short breathing spell.

"What's with you, Vasia, you nodding your head? Didn't you get enough sleep last night?" Mitrakova the engineer speaks to the young form man.

48

"Didn't sleep at all last night. Took my wife to the maternity ward. "

"Congratulations. But why didn't you tell anyone? "

"What's there to talk about? Wanted a son and got a daughter. "

Tamara Dmitrievna speaks reproachfully:

"You fool, you, Vasilii. Look--I'm a woman. Do I work any worse than you? "

"Wait a minute, Dmitrievna! You're alright, tops with us. I didn't mean it that way. " The young father tries with some embarrassment to set things right.

Other workers come up and congratulate the fellow. He cheers up. The girl's name is Svetlana.

"Thanks, Tamara Dmitrievna, " he says softly, after everyone has gone on about his business.

The subway builders respect engineer Mitrakova. They not only pay attention to her just and pithy words at meetings, they come to get advice from her on family matters. Everyone knows her. Returning sixteen years ago from the Transcarpathian area, she went to work on the construction of the Leningrad subway. There is not a tunnel or a station where Mitrakova has not worked.

When the form-setting machinery and the muck loaders began to appear in the shafts, the subway cadres were the first to make use of the new technology.

"Let's have a look at the assembly, " said the mechanic V. T. Kulikov to the tunnel worker Mitrakova, "You're going to work on the machine. "

And Tamara Dmitrievna, after finishing her shift at the shaft, didn't leave the rig. She learned every nut and bolt. Now she can handle any repair job if necessary. Running the form-jumbo, Mitrakova has earned the title of leading worker. And she has come into her worker's glory: they presented her with the Order of the Banner of Red Labor.

The trees slumber, wrapped in their white hoar frost. People are coming home from work. At that very moment Mitrakova is descending into shaft number 315. There, deep under the earth, they are outfitting the station for Leo Tolstoy Place. Up above, lights are going on in the windows, children are falling off to sleep in their little beds. But here, tirelessly, the iron hand of the form-jumbo moves, guided by the engineer Mitrakova. They are building the tunnel.

Engineer Mitrakova has been elected deputy twice to the Frunzenskii City-<u>raion</u> Soviet. She tries to help people with everything; she can't imagine a life without social activity.

And then the day came when this modest worker was named at a pre-election meeting which nominated candidates to the Supreme Soviet of the Russian Federation.

"Why such an honor for me, why such faith?" Mitrakova asked as she came to the brigade. She looked at the brigadier Vasilii Kalinin, at the shift engineer Aleksei Kuznetsov, at the form man Aleksei Ulitkin.

Ulitkin answered for all: "We believe in you, Tamara Dmitrievna!"

The above article contains most of the characteristics of a type of literature which is highly, drearily standardized. From it and from many others like it, certain general characteristics of the ideal candidate emerge. The candidate is selected because he or she is a leading, powerful personality; in the case of Mitrakova, there is indeed something extraordinary about the woman's career. The candidate has authority among her peers because she has earned it in difficult circumstances. And this is the point: The deputy is supposed to be a respected leaders, but not because this makes him a good legislator--for the Soviet deputy is not supposed to legislate. He is supposed to help secure acceptance of whatever program the regime may be pushing. By their example, deputies are expected to facilitate execution of policy, not legislation and formulation of policy. This is why high caliber candidates are chosen carefully in the advance meetings. This is why deputies are often truly remarkable people. They become symbols of the regime at the local level, and for this reason the regime seeks the best people.

The ideals held up for the candidate are partly those of the society, partly those required by the political system. Following are some of the characteristics of the good candidate and deputy:

In relation to his job or profession:

The candidate gives the impression that work is the key to personal salvation and to social advancement. The regime asks first of all that the person work hard, conscientiously, and well. The best workers are rewarded by being made deputies.

Thus the candidate tends to be a shock worker or an innovator.

He works without mistakes and consistently overfulfills his plan quota.

He is possessed of an inner compulsion to work harder and better.

If the candidate is older, born in tsarist times, then he has come a long way from poverty and oppression, through study and hard work, to a position of respect in the new Soviet society.

If the person is a professional or creative worker, he has a compulsion to excellence. He is a thinker.

He is generous with his knowledge and his time; he has a highly developed sense of duty to his job and he knows he must help others develop this attitude. He assists others, the younger workers, in developing not only productivity, but also a love for the job. Moving examples of this are cited for the benefit of new candidates.

For example, one railway worker, a candidate, spent his days off at the round-house, telling young engineers how to run a train on time.

In regard to his personal characteristics:

He is a quiet, modest person whose inner warmth communicates itself (this is the official image; in fact he may be a blatant bore).

He has the respect of his fellows; he leads rather than drives. He is a real person, a "chelovek."

The social consciousness of the candidate is highly developed and he is a leader in various social organizations.

In short, these are the qualities of a natural leader, one who can most easily set an example for his fellows in the execution of given tasks. The newspapers tell us exactly why the "best people" are chosen to be deputies.

"Bourgeois" Elections

An important part of Soviet campaign and other literature is aimed at demonstrating the superiority of the Soviet system of democracy by discrediting political processes in the West. This starts at the top and runs down through the order of writers to the pamphleteer and journalist. Criticism of the West is part of the official policy of the party and government. A section of the new Party Program devoted to the "Crisis of World Capitalism" includes comments on the allegedly anti-democratic character of "bourgeois" electoral systems.[7] The theme was used by Khrushchev at the XXII Party Congress, where he said that deception of the masses and the policeman's club are the real weapons in the West's arsenal of democracy,[8] and again in his campaign speech in 1963.[9] It is the duty of a Soviet scholar to expose the evils of Western "democracy,"[10] and university textbooks on government devote sections to criticism of the bourgeois world. In the widely used book of Professor Lepeshkin, for example, the concluding chapter of each part of the work is devoted to attacks on Western politics and government.[11]

During the election campaign, pamphleteers and journalists stress this line. The brochures on Soviet elections which appear in book store displays devote much space to attacking the Western parliamentary systems.[12] The fact that such themes appear is not surprising, but the quantity of the material is. In a reference work on electoral systems of the world, the ten pages devoted to the USA are one long criticism of American politics;[13] in the handbook for the Soviet voter published for the 1963 elections, a third of the book does not concern Soviet elections at all, but rather the evils of Western, and chiefly American, practices of representative government.[14]

All this writing is highly repetitious. The principal themes can be expressed succinctly in a few lines:

Bourgeois electoral systems are not democratic because they are not representative. Capital controls the elections, the workers and farmers don't influence the legislatures, and the will of the people is thwarted by the monopolists behind the scenes who manipulate the reactionary national, state, and local bodies.

The majority system of voting allows minority candidates, those with less than 50 per cent of the total vote to be elected (such a practice is forbidden by the Soviet statute), and this is undemocratic.

The voters have no voice in the nomination of candidates!

Terror, bribery, swindling, and cheating are component parts of all Western elections.

Various kinds of voting qualifications, e.g., literacy, residence, property, race and education, prevent a large proportion of the electorate, especially Negroes, from ever getting to the polls. These qualifications are set up by the monopolists as a means of strengthening their hold on the country.

Really progressive forces such as the Communists are, for all practical purposes, disfranchised.

These are the main points of attack on Western politics, repeated over and over again with variations and elaborations, statistics, and pictures. As election day comes nearer, the local journalists take up the subject with greater frequency and the papers devote long articles to the evils of the Western world. [15] This particular phenomenon is of interest not because of the content of the material presented, for it is highly tendentious and uninteresting, but because the Soviet Government feels a need to devote such a sizable portion of its own election literature to denigrating the West.

Meetings and Instructions

The voter has two possible direct involvements in the pre-election process. One is the candidate's meeting with voters, and the other is a visit from an agitator. Since nominees must be registered within twenty or fifteen days of the election, depending on whether they are candidates for republic or local offices, the meetings with voters begin about this time. Reports of such meet-

ings began to appear in the newspapers about February 15, 1963,

a little ahead of the required time, [16] and they continued right up

to the eve of election day. Every candidate is supposed to meet at

least once with the voters of his district.

These meetings bring the candidates to the voters and bring

the complaints and instructions of the voters to the candidates. It

is the first opportunity during the campaign for the voters to express

themselves. While the meetings with republic candidates tend to

preserve a rigidly formal atmosphere, the meetings with the

candidates to lower level soviets of the city and city-raion may end

in a flood of give-and-take from the floor. It is here that people

may rise and tell their representatives what is troubling them. For

the first time in the election process one can observe a meeting of

real interest, thanks to the rare factor of spontaneity.

The organization of both is the responsibility of the party

organs specializing in mass work; it is largely their job to get the

space, provide the entertainment, and get the crowds out to the

meetings.

The first type of meeting, the large one for an RSFSR

candidate, is furnished with a brass band, with speakers, and usually with some form of entertainment afterwards. In many ways it is similar to the nomination meetings except that the candidate is present and delivers a short speech (he is usually not present at this nomination). The meetings are arranged for the evening, as a rule, and last approximately an hour. A large part of the program is devoted to speeches about the policies and plans of the party and government, and are full of high praise and promise for both. Because of the formal, ceremonial nature of these meetings, probably no one will speak from the floor with instructions for the candidate. And in keeping with the solemn atmosphere on such occasions, the meetings often close with an eloquently worded letter full of resolve and respect to the First Secretary and the Central Committee of the party.

Meetings with candidates to lower level soviets have a different flavor altogether. These are usually small, less formal, with perhaps one speech by the candidate's sworn supporter and with much discussion from the audience. They are neighborhood meetings, held during the evening in an agitpunkt, club, or similar place. Conversation may develop on concrete issues at a lively tempo.

The chairman of the meeting is perhaps a party organizational worker, or the head of some other social organization such as a house committee. A tally is kept of instructions and of the persons making them; they become part of the record of business of the soviet, and an attempt is made to keep a count on the number of instructions received and the number fulfilled during each two year session.[17] In Soviet journals and brochures, considerable space is devoted to the subject of voters' instructions, for in theory one of the main tasks of the deputy and his soviet is to hear and respond to the voice of the people as expressed in the instructions. The fulfillment of them is a quantitative gauge for the Soviet degree of democracy.

Following is a sample of a meeting held for candidates to the city and city-raion soviets, reconstructed from notes taken while attending several of them. Candidates to the two soviets are meeting some voters at an agitpunkt; after they have been introduced and a couple of brief biographical sketches presented, the chairman speaks:

> Chairman: Would anyone like to address the candidates?
>
> 1st Voter: Can you remodel the movie house out here?
>
> Chairman: What is your name and address?

1st Voter: (Calls out his name and address; the secretary makes a note.)

2nd Voter: I'd like to get the housing office to send a man out to fix my roof. Pretty soon it's going to be spring and the water will start pouring in.

3rd Voter: I think you ought to get the shops next to our apartment building to move. They work there three shifts a day, and they make so much noise that we can't sleep. We have to work too.

Candidate: That is a pretty difficult request.

Former Deputy: Do you mind if I interrupt here? During the last session of the soviet we also took up this matter, which was one of the instructions given us by the voters two years ago. We went to our City-raion Soviet, to the City Soviet, and finally to the regional Council of the National Economy. Plans have been made to remove the shop to the outskirts of the city during the current Seven Year Plan. It will be done eventually.

Chairman: Comrade, you have to understand why this situation exists. The shops were built when the city was small. At that time there were no apartment houses around. But you can see that the shops just can't be moved overnight. It is a very expensive undertaking.

3rd Voter: Yes, I see that. Well, I just wanted to mention it, because it does bother us.

4th Voter: Can't you get the bus route changed so that it doesn't run past the hospital? All the dust it stirs up and the noise of the traffic make things uncomfortable for the sick people.

Chairman: This request is being considered by the Transportation Board of the City Soviet. It is out of our hands.

5th Voter: I want to ask you about my pension. I moved here from Kazakhstan and I'm not getting my full allotment.

Chairman: This is a legal question, Comrade, and you had better go to a lawyer for consultation. Now let me remind you other comrades to limit your requests to matters of principle, to questions which have meaning for all the citizens of the area. This is not the place for personal requests.

6th Voter: We want a place for a club in our apartment house. We need a room to watch television.

Candidate: You really should take this up with your house committee or housing office, but I'll try to help you on the matter. Make sure you get your name and address into the protocol.

7th Voter: There are too many people in our apartment,

and I've been trying for three years to get some of them moved out. There are more people than the rules allow.

8th Voter: Our apartment house is an old one, with a kitchen that was installed where a storeroom used to be. Many families use the one kitchen and children are always playing in the hall next to it. But there is no window in the kitchen itself. What I'm afraid of is that someday the gas will be left on and it will be fatal for the little ones.

9th Voter (an older woman): There is something that's been bothering me since two elections ago. That little stand which sells beer on the corner is an eyesore. A bunch of rowdies and drunks are always standing around there, and they set a bad example for the school children in the neighborhood. Besides, there are foreigners in the area and they should not see this sort of thing.

Voice (not completely sober): You old women just don't like to see men drink. You don't understand that we need a drink. You don't know what fun is anyway-- all you can do is save up your kopeks.

9th Voter: Go ahead and drink if you want. All I want is for them to move the beer stand around to a back street where people won't see it.

Chairman: I think we can close the meeting now. We

have given our candidates enough to work on this session.

The meeting is over, but the people go on talking in small groups which only slowly disperse. It has been an interesting session, the main feature of which is the immediate, local, rather unimportant nature of the problems discussed. No vital policy issues are raised. What the people ask for are minor improvements in conditions close at hand. Housing matters are frequently touched on, because they are an issue which receives much official attention and one which can be safely discussed. We also see that it very often takes a long time, months or even years, for requests to be acted on.

For the Westerner, the meeting is a curious one. It is not political in the meaning of a discussion of policies. The meeting deals with minor inadequacies in the execution, not formation, of plans. The goals and policies of the government are accepted at the outset; what the people are asking for is a solution to problems which in the last analysis have been created by the government. For example, most of the requests center around questions of housing. But these questions tend to arise precisely because the government mismanages its monopoly on housing. And when the public meeting gives people a chance to express themselves on the issue, this is interpreted by the Soviet publicists as an achievement of Soviet democracy. It is democratic, so their thinking runs, to let people grumble a bit about the problems which have been created for them.

The Agitator

Because the Sovet election is mainly a gesture of mass approval of the government and its plans, the work of the agitator is especially important. This is the person who makes the face to face contact with each individual voter, enumerates policies and plans, and solicits a personal commitment to participate in the process by voting. Higher party organizers know just as well as any American advertising man that face to face contact is most important, and agitators are sent out in great numbers. For example, the Leninskii City-raion reported 5,000 agitators at work as early as January 11;[18] on March 1, two days before the election, the Vyborgskii City-raion indicated that 10,000 agitators were busy in that area alone.[19]

The party is responsible for organizing the work of the agitators. It does so chiefly by reaching down the chain of command to all kinds of public organizations which are asked to supply the needed agitators from their members. One newspaper stated that some 450,000 persons were enrolled in various social organizations in Leningrad and suggested that all be put to work in the campaign.[20] Another paper gives a more conservative figure, indicating that in the Leningrad oblast there were some 100,000 persons in voluntary organizations.[21] In either event, this is a massive reserve of volunteers who can be called into election work.

Housing offices not only furnish some of the space for election offices and meetings but sometimes organize their own activist groups.[22] One such office put twenty-nine agitators into the field.[23] Aside from this, each office most likely has its own room or corner of a room for political agitation, the "red corner," where political literature is always available. A newspaper account describes a question and answer period held in a room maintained by the 16th Housing Office of the Moskovskii City-raion. At this meeting, the principal figures in attendance were the chairmen of the city-raion soviet, the leader of the deputy group (a relatively new type organization composed of all the deputies from various soviets who live in one area), and some members of the city-raion branch of the Society for the Dissemination of Political and Scientific

Knowledge. They spoke with the voters, told them about plans for the enormous building program in the city-raion, and answered some fifty questions.[24] According to the same newspaper account, "More than 150 requests [for such question and answer periods] were made to the district committee of the Communist Party of the Soviet Union. The agitpunkts are supplied with standing groups of speakers by the district party committee and by the Executive Committee of the city-raion soviet. In this group there are more than 120 party and soviet workers."

The persons in charge of such activities, i.e., of the activist groups, agitpunkts, and editors of wall newspapers, are approved by the city-raion party organization.[25] Another newspaper reported that the city party committee organized agitators and instructed them in the principal themes which they were to carry to the voters: increasing the productivity of labor, achieving new successes in technology, and fulfilling the goals of the Seven Year Plan.[26] This will strike the Westerner as a strongly pro-government platform, one which ignores the desires of the voter.

Under ideal circumstances, each agitator visits about ten apartments, which brings him in contact with ten to thirty families, depending on how crowded the quarters are. He is supposed to speak to each family or apartment group, and leave with them a printed slip of paper giving the name of the candidates from the given district. If he is slack in his work, he may leave the printed notices in mail boxes without making the personal calls. During the course of the conversation, the agitator not only explains the aims and accomplishments of the government, he not only "sells" the government to the people, he also solicits complaints and divides them on the spot into ills which are being remedied, can be remedied, or cannot be remedied.

The following newspaper account[27] gives a picture of a model visit to an apartment:

A Heart to Heart Talk

There it is, the apartment in the large, bright new house on Gavanskaia Street. On the door--one bell for all. That means the neighbors here get along well, the agitator from Sevkabel [factory], Ivan Romanovich Gritsai, says to himself as he rings the bell.

It is not the first time Gritsai has been an agitator. Once again in the homes on Gavanskaia, once again at apartment 29. When meeting people for the first time, the agitator wants to find some words from the heart for his conversation. He wants to be a welcome guest.

To do this he thoroughly prepares himself. First of all it

67

is necessary to talk about the way things are going in your own neighborhood.

And these things are gratifying. The decisions of the November Plenum of the Central Committee of the CPSU have inspired the residents of Vasilevskii Island, as they have all Soviet people, to new achievements in labor. At the Elektroapparat Factory they just lately tried out some new 750,000 kilowatt transformers. The shipbuilders of the Baltiiskii Factory have taken on the obligation to build, ahead of schedule, some new giant tankers during the fifth year of the 7 Year Plan. The textile worker from the Vera Slutskaia Factory decided to turn out 10,000 meters more than the plan calls for of dress material.

It will also be interesting for the voters to know how things stand in regard to housing. The agitator Gritsai has the following data ready: Last year on Vasilevskii Island, 50,000 square meters of housing space were begun, and major repairs on about 27,000 square meters. Next year they are going to begin reconstructing old areas. On the sites of little homes, great, bright buildings will rise, some of them twenty stories high. They are beginning to construct a new subway line which will connect Srednyi Prospekt with the center of town. The area is being converted to gas.

It is pleasant to mention such facts in a chat. All families have been put on the lists [for new housing] where there is less than 4-1/2 square meters per person. At the present time, all persons who have been on the lists since 1958 are receiving new apartments.

... The agitator rings. An elderly lady in an apron opens the door.

68

"Hello," says Gritsai, "I am your agitator and I'd like to get acquainted with the voters."

"Kuk'ianova," the woman introduces herself. "Please come in. We are always happy to have guests. I'll call the other residents right away."

Three families live in apartment 29. This evening almost all of them are home--the lathe operator S. G. Nedorubkov and his wife Vera Ivanovna, a teacher, the electrician German Perov, and Kuk'ianova. Only the wife of Perov, a worker at the factory Voskhod, is not there yet. But she should be along soon.

"Well, shall we begin our chat?" Gritsai thinks, meeting the people.

"Oh, what are we standing in the kitchen for," Luk'ianova throws up her hands. "Please come into my room," she cheerfully invites the agitator and her neighbors. "I have room for you all."

In a cozy, bright room the lively, soulful conversation gets started by itself.

First of all, the agitator acquaints the residents with the biographies of the candidates to the Supreme Soviet of the RSFSR and to the local soviets, for whom they will be voting on March 3.

The name of Anna Arsent'evna Gritskevich, a worker at the Sevkabel Factory whom they have named as their candidate to the Leningrad City Soviet, is well known to them all. The fame of her deeds long since passed far beyond the confines of Vasilevskii Island. That name is famous throughout the country.

"In times past," Gritsai recalls, "Anna Arsent'evna was the first to begin the struggle for a solicitous use of non-ferrous metals, and introduced the personal account into the system. And now in our city alone more than 13,000 persons are following the example of this notable worker."

The residents ask him to give some details about the candidate to the Supreme Soviet of the RSFSR, Iurii Zinov'evich Rybakov of the Baltiiskii Factory.

"This profound manifestation of confidence [his nomination] was earned by the machinist through his own selfless work. Rybakov holds dearly the honor of his factory and his profession. This remarkable person has time for everything--for education, for social work. The people at the Baltiiskii are convinced that he will be a worthy representative of the working class in the Soviet parliament."

Some of the facts which he had stored up on the way to his friends came in handy for Gritsai.

Many things interested the residents--both the building prospects for the district and the growth of service facilities.

It was a heart to heart discussion in the apartment, lasting late into the evening.

Then it was time to go. The agitator invited the people to drop around to the agitpunkt on Vesel'naia Street. "The whole apartment will come," the residents said.

"I'll be back in a few days--if you don't object, of course," says Gritsai, smiling.

"You're welcome," Luk'ianova answers for all.

Going out into the frosty air, Ivan Romanovich does not hurry as he goes to the bus stop. He thinks with satisfaction about the way his first meeting turned out to be an exceptional success.

The above article tells many things about the work of the agitator. First of all, he walks a two-way street: he not only promises people things, he quite candidly solicits certain commitments from the electorate--to participate in the election, and to increase their labor efforts. As party propaganda tells the people, the abundance on which communism will depend can be achieved only if they in return, or in advance, give greater effort to the aims and programs of the party and government.

The article quoted here resembles much Soviet journalism in that it was not written primarily as a piece of reporting. It was a model for the agitators who in the next few days started canvassing the apartments of Leningrad. Barely below the surface of this heartwarming incident are general instructions for agitators:

The agitator should be well equipped with facts about current policies and programs of the party and government. He should have data on hand, e.g., about the number of square meters of housing space built already and yet to be built. The promise is important.

The meeting should be a soulful one, with emotions and words coming directly from the heart.

The agitator should be acquainted with the biography of the candidate he is propagandizing.

The work of the agitator provides important spiritual rewards.

Election Day

The polling places, each of which serves two or three districts in a local election, are set up in agitpunkts, schools, Palaces of Culture, or other convenient public places. The room for balloting is usually prepared a few days before the Sunday of the election, outfitted with velvet covered tables, red bunting, and a conspicuously locked ballot box. It may also be decorated with flowers, pictures of Central Committee members, Lenin everywhere, and on election day itself there are sometimes refreshments plus a brass band intermittently playing martial music. Liquor is obtainable in stores and bars. Red banners display current slogans in large white letters. Some voting places are decorated more imaginatively, revealing the work of many careful hands.

The polls are open from 6 a. m. until midnight. On duty is the head of the precinct commission, plus several volunteer helpers who pass out and later count the ballots. Machine voting seems to

72

be unheard of. The voter enters the polling place and goes to the section of the long green table which is marked with his letter of the alphabet. There he shows an identification document and receives his ballots (three of them in Leningrad). Care must be taken that he is given the correct set of ballots for his district, but this is the responsibility of the volunteer workers, whose task is made easier by the fact that the ballots come in different sizes and colors according to regulations published by the Central Election Commission of the RSFSR[28] (a facsimile of a ballot is shown in Appendix K). His name is checked off the list of voters. There are no control numbers on the ballots.

The voter can then step into a booth to mark the ballot if he wishes, for the statute requires that this be available. However, only a few people utilize this opportunity. The ballot does not even have to be marked; the statute says that a voter only has to "leave on each ballot the name of the candidate he is voting for, crossing out the names of the rest. "[29] If the ballot has only one name on it--as did all the ballots in the city of Leningrad, he has merely to drop it in the urn and his voting is done. So the great majority of them pick up their ballots, ceremoniously walk the length of the room, deposit them in the urn without even looking at them, and leave. In some precincts a member of the Pioneer Youth Organiza-tion, dressed up in a white shirt and red neckerchief, salutes them at the urn. That's all there is to voting--no choices, decisions, or questions.

The newspapers appearing on election day provide a con-venient summary of the major themes involved. Judging from the treatment it receives in the mass media, election day ranks right after November 7 and May Day in national political significance. It even brings out a poetic flair in journalists when they attach such epithets as "harbinger of spring" to it. Or as one journalist, dwell-ing on the grandiose achievements of the Soviet regime, had to exclaim, "O brave new world..."[30]

The official attitude toward the elections is capsulized in the headlines, some of which are worth noting: "Everyone to the Polls!"--"Day of Unity of the Folk and Party and Government"--"Spring Outside, Spring in Your Hearts!"--"For Peace, Happiness, Communism!"--"Solicitude for the Soviet People" (referring to Khrushchev's election speech)--"The Folk, Master of the Country"--"Russia, My Motherland"--"In the Service of the People"--"A Just Man" (referring to a candidate). In a two party system, election season is the time for thoroughgoing criticism of the policies of the

74

government. In the Soviet Union, with its single party system, the opposite is true. Policies may be reviewed and plans presented, but they are all approved (even if it is the policy of disapproving, such as de-Stalinization). One Soviet writer says that voting is a "deed appraising the activities of the Soviet government in the past and defining its program in the future,"[31] but the line between appraising and praising is indistinct.

Why should the Soviet citizens be grateful to his government and to the party? The government press supplies the answer in its review of forty-odd years of history: The Soviet regime smashed the oppressive rule of the tsars and landlords, held the imperialist armies at bay when the country was weak, and made it possible to found a just government of, by and for the workers and peasants. In World War II they (almost single-handedly) ended the Fascist control of Europe. Now they are modernizing Russia, giving away things like apartments, a larger share of culture, and more free time. And they are ahead of the Americans in launching people into space. The debt from the past is enormous. The one from the future is incalculable--for it will bring communism, the era of plenty. Only the most insensitive clod, the most ungrateful recalcitrant, could fail to be moved by the infinite care bestowed on the people by the government and party. And this thought too is expressed in an election day banner, "Citizens, be worthy of the solicitude which the Party surrounds you with." Voting is an expression of gratitude for this omnipresent care.

The 99 Per Cent Vote

Aware that the selection of candidates is managed, and knowing that the ballots carry only one name and that the elections are not a contest in the Western sense, a person is justified in asking whether 99 per cent of the people really go out and vote, and if so, why? Sometimes the voting statistics do seem to be falsified (as one Leningrad volunteer put it, when the ballot counters turn up with more than 100 per cent of the ballots in the box, then you know that someone has been working too zealously on his election norm). Nevertheless, the overwhelming percentage of eligible voters cast their ballots regularly.

The important question to be answered in regard to a Soviet election is this: Whom does one vote for? Russians vote for the Soviet regime. And if casting a vote on election day is a sign of support of the regime, then not casting a vote is a sign of opposition. So if the Russian is asked, in effect, whether he is voting "for" or "against" the party and the government, he doesn't even have to think. He votes "for. " Voting is both a patriotic and a social activity, invested with the diverse pleasures which most people derive from performing a commendable action. It is not an onerous duty. On the contrary, it can be a source of satisfaction.

In addition to these intangibles, an elaborate machinery has been created to increase the total vote. Local party organs keep a running tabulation of the vote on election day. In Leningrad, for example, the precincts phone in their results to party headquarters every two hours. The percentage of persons who have already voted is calculated and released to the radio.[32] By midafternoon the percentages are already in the nineties.

If a signal comes into party headquarters that the citizens in a given precinct are not voting in the required numbers, corrective steps can be taken immediately. Party organizers, agitators, the police if necessary may be brought into action. We recall from the description of the voting procedure that as each person comes in and gets his ballot, his name is checked off the list of voters. This list tells who has voted. And it also gives the name and address of everyone in the precinct who has not voted. For those who have not appeared by mid-afternoon, telephones, automobiles, and personnel are ready: Someone will appear at the person's apartment to remind him that it is his duty to get down to the polls. This is usually effective, for if the citizen still refuses to vote after such a visit, his action can be construed as enmity toward the regime, and there are not many in the USSR who wish to go on record as entertaining such an attitude. This arrangement brings out many people who would stay home out of sheer indifference.

For those who know they are going to be travelling on election day, elaborate provisions are made. Before leaving his place of residence, the traveller is supposed to present himself at the temporary office where the lists of voters are kept. Here he asks for an absentee voter's certificate.[33] His name is checked off the voting list, and he receives a piece of paper which entitles him to vote at any polling place, even if it is in a neighboring republic. If he is on a train, he can vote in a special car set up for that purpose.[34] In this case he votes for the candidate of the precinct in which he happens to find himself, and not for those representing his own domicile. Whom he votes for is not important. Important only is the fact that he does vote.

To assist the bedridden, election workers are authorized to carry a sealed urn to the invalid's apartment so that he can vote there.[35] Provisions are made for an even more unusual case: Suppose that a person is travelling across the city and falls ill just before election day. He would not have the absentee voter's certificate, since he did not expect to fall ill; and he cannot return to his precinct because the illness has immobilized him. Still he can vote. Official automobiles are assigned to precinct supervisors for a day, and can be used to go across town and pick up this ballot for deposit in its own precinct.

In this far-reaching, compulsive effort to get everyone to register approval of the regime, almost all eventualities have been prepared for in advance. And still there must be a few people who do not want to vote--not the sick, the travelling, or the indifferent, but those who simply do not wish to register approval of the regime. Indeed, it would be a strange society which didn't produce such people. Do they exist in the USSR? The following conversations suggest that they do, but that most of them also vote.

The following, in question and answer form, is an account of some residents of one apartment house, part of which was heard in a conversation at a polling place and part of which came in the form of an anecdote:

Q: Elections in the USSR impress Westerners. The overwhelming majority of Russians have come out to vote, and now by mid-afternoon more than 90 per cent have already cast their ballots. But still I wonder: Don't some people ever vote <u>against</u> the candidates?

A: Sometimes it does happen that people scratch the name off the ballot. It occurs more often out in the villages.

Q: Does this invalidate the ballot?

A: Yes.

Q: Can persons step into the booth and write in the name of a candidate?

A: Of course a person can do this. But it also invalidates the ballot. You see, a candidate has to be nominated by an organization, approved in advance, and registered according to the statute.

Q: So a write-in would not be valid?

A: It would be meaningless. You can't elect anyone with a write-in vote.

Q: Perhaps this explains why few people make use of the voting booths with the curtains hanging in front of them. It looks like about one person in ten is getting into there.

A: More people go into them now than during the time of the cult of personality [the Stalin era]. In those days, someone was keeping track of the people who went into the booths. We don't do that any more.

Q: Don't some people stay away from the polls altogether? Aren't there any people who just refuse to vote? I can't believe that in any country 100 per cent of the people are totally for the government. That would be an unhealthy sign, don't you think?

A: I heard of a case where some people decided they would not vote. They wanted to make a protest about their housing conditions.

Q: What was the trouble?

A: Several families were living in one of the older apartments. Last fall some workmen from the housing office came to fix the plumbing. Well, they cut a hole in the roof of one of the rooms used by all the residents, but when they finished the job they did not patch up the hole.

Q: It was thirty below last winter.

A: It was cold.

Q: What did they do about it?

A: The residents called the housing office and asked them to come and fix the roof. When this got no results, they called the Executive Committee of of their city-raion soviet. No help. So they called up their deputy.

Q: Was he able to do anything?

A: No, the matter dragged on for months.

Q: There must have been some way they could have gotten the roof repaired. That isn't much of a job.

A: A minor job, but it became a matter of principle: Of course, they could have given the workmen a bottle or two of vodka and it would have been fixed before they left. But these people wanted to settle the matter honestly. Bribery is not a good thing.

Q: So on election day they decided they would not go to the polls?

A: No, they told the agitator who came to visit them that they were not going to vote unless the roof had been fixed by Saturday, the day before the election. This was an ultimatum.

Q: What could the agitator do?

A: First he had to get over his shock. It was an unusual experience for him. But he called the housing office and told them to get a repairman over there right away.

Q: Did that do the job?

A: No, when Sunday morning came, the hole was still there.

Q: Did they vote?

A: Naturally they voted.

Q: Wasn't the atmosphere a bit tense when they showed up at the polls?

A: It may have been. I heard that the volunteer workers at the precinct gave them special attention when they came in, asking them with perhaps a bit of ambiguity how things were at home. The residents simply put it this way: Is a little hole in the roof any reason to be against the Soviet regime? Of course not.

Q: And so they all voted?

A: They voted, to a man. The roof is still not repaired.

Q: But what if they really had refused to come out to the polls, what would you do in a case like that?

A: I wouldn't do anything. But I would begin to think, now why is this person against the government? Yes, I'd want to investigate the matter.

4

SUMMARY CONTENTS

The direct cost of Soviet elections is minimal, in compari-

son to American elections infinitesimal. It is borne by the govern-

ment.[1] According to one member of an Executive Committee in

Leningrad, a city-raion spends about one hundred rubles (approxi-

mately $111.00 in 1963) for the election. Most of this goes into

signs for the precincts and districts, and for printing ballots and

lists of candidates. Newspaper space and radio time are not in-

cluded in the figure, nor are the wages of personnel in the party

and administrative apparatus who devote full or part time to the

campaign. The heads of precinct commissions are freed from

their regular work two weeks so they can devote all their time to

the election, so this too would have to be added to the expense.[2]

But in general there are few paid workers.

The candidate, of course, spends nothing on getting

elected. He is drafted for the job, and drafting him is a govern-

ment responsibility. While the post is supposed to be an honor, it is also a burden. There are no pecuniary rewards, nor does the position give power over the administration. And so it is doubtful that most people would pay for their nomination to a soviet even if they thought it would help.

The party unit which plays a key role in the election process is the Department of Propaganda and Agitation. The work is difficult and time-consuming and it requires the services of a capable organizer. The head of this department has the main responsibility for planning the meetings for selecting candidates, nominating them, and introducing them to the voters. He has to find the space and arrange for entertainment and refreshments. He organizes the work of the agitators, arranges for press releases and for many other details. At the lower levels he works almost single-handedly. Success or failure of the campaign lies largely with this man of the party apparatus.

The administrative side of the elections, especially registration and balloting, is handled by the government. Specifically, this is up to the secretary of the Executive Committee, to the General Department, and to the Organization-Instructions Department of a given soviet. It is their job to instruct campaign workers in handling documents and managing polling places, and to assist

the members of election commissions. At the city-raion level,
this amounts to five or six employees who devote part of their
time to the job.

When the exercise is all over, the regime once again has
enlisted a fresh mass of people whose job it is to improve the
efficiency of Soviet government. The candidate is not selected by
the people. The deputy has no legal power to formulate policy. [3]
He is primarily an intermediary between the government and the
people. To assist the government, he plays the role of an organizer,
one who encourages others to fulfill the current tasks defined by
the party; and so he has to be one of the "best people." From the
other side, he channels grievances from the people to the proper
authorities, so that the programs of party and government will be
carried out more efficiently. But these programs are in the last
analysis determined by the party and to a much lesser extent by
the permanent officials of the Executive Committees. The work of
the deputy, according to Soviet writers, is an outstanding example
of their democracy. It is in fact difficult to describe the arrangement as being even political, if that term is related in some way
to the formulation of public policy.

When the Russians vote, they put their seal of approval on

86

the entire arrangement. They never turn out one government and bring in a new. They do not even vote for alternative policies or competing candidates. They vote for the Soviet regime.

APPENDICES

NOTES

GLOSSARY

Administrative–Territorial Structure of the USSR, 1963

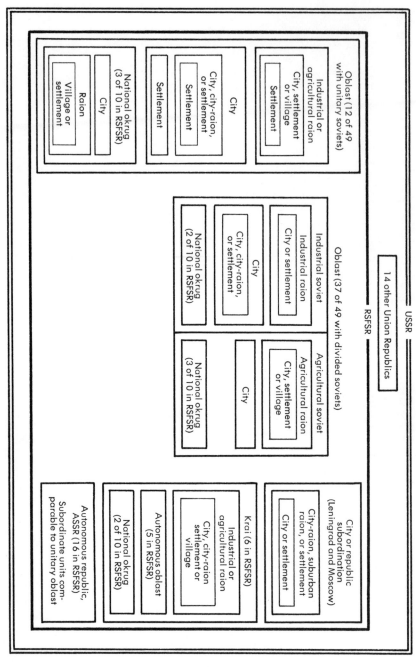

APPENDIX A

Notes

The chart shows schematically the most typical administrative structures of the USSR, and particularly of the RSFSR; in the other fourteen constituent republics, the administrative structure is similar but generally less complex.

Each box on the chart represents one administrative-territorial unit, and at the same time the soviet of that unit. In those boxes where the name of more than one type of unit is found, the unit may possibly, but not necessarily, exist; this depends on the locality in question.

To find the number of soviets standing above a given administrative-territorial unit, count the number of boxes surrounding it; the resulting figure is the number of deputies directly elected from that unit. The totals come to five, six, or seven, depending on the administrative unit.

The USSR is represented by a double line to account for the bicameral Supreme Soviet of the USSR.

The term "settlement" is used collectively to represent three different types:

workers' settlement	(rabochii poselok)
resort settlement	(kurortnyi poselok)
country cottage settlement	(dachnyi poselok)

These settlements are discussed in David L'vovich Zlatopol'skii, Gosudarstvennoe ustroistvo SSSR (Moscow: Gosiurizdat), 1960, pp. 287-88.

Sources

SSSR. Administrativno-territorial'noe delenie Soiuznykh respublik, na 1 aprelia 1963 g. (Mokva: Izd-vo "Izvestiia," 1963). 575 pp.

"Ob izmeneniakh v administrativno-territorial'nom delenii, " Vedemosti Verkhovnogo Soveta SSSR (no. 12, Mar. 20, 1963), pp. 207-83. The basic document setting up the dual system of soviets.

Further charts on the electoral system of Russia and the USSR will be found in:

Carson, George Barr Jr. Electoral Practices in the U.S.S.R. (New York: Frederick A. Praeger, 1955). 151 pp.

Denisov, A., and M. Kirichenko. Soviet State Law, trans. by S. Belskii and M. Saifulin (Moscow: Foreign Languages Publishing House, 1960), pp. 168-69.

City and Suburban Raions of Leningrad, 1963

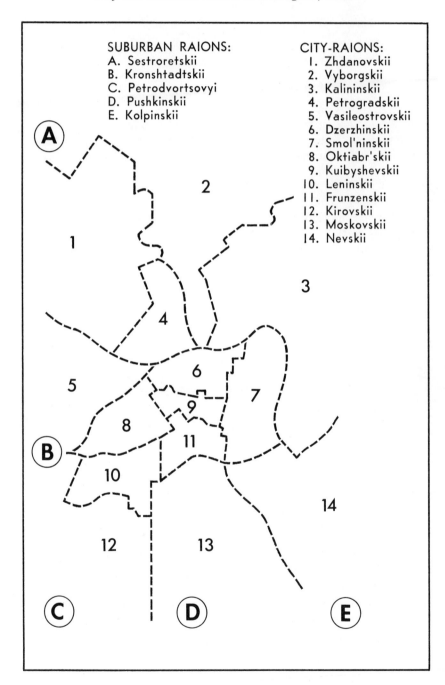

SUBURBAN RAIONS:
A. Sestroretskii
B. Kronshtadtskii
C. Petrodvortsovyi
D. Pushkinskii
E. Kolpinskii

CITY-RAIONS:
1. Zhdanovskii
2. Vyborgskii
3. Kalininskii
4. Petrogradskii
5. Vasileostrovskii
6. Dzerzhinskii
7. Smol'ninskii
8. Oktiabr'skii
9. Kuibyshevskii
10. Leninskii
11. Frunzenskii
12. Kirovskii
13. Moskovskii
14. Nevskii

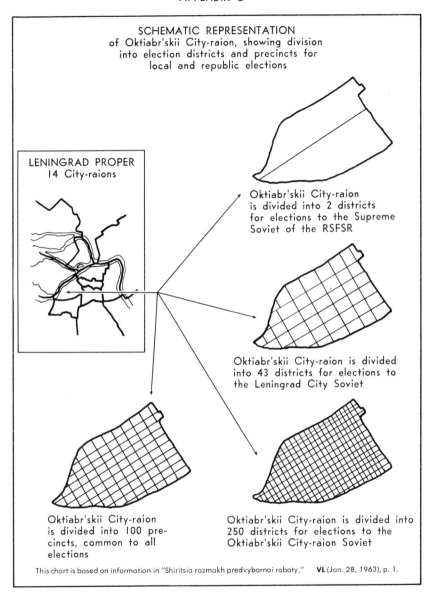

SCHEMATIC REPRESENTATION
of Oktiabr'skii City-raion, showing division
into election districts and precincts for
local and republic elections

LENINGRAD PROPER
14 City-raions

Oktiabr'skii City-raion
is divided into 2 districts
for elections to the Supreme
Soviet of the RSFSR

Oktiabr'skii City-raion is divided
into 43 districts for elections to
the Leningrad City Soviet

Oktiabr'skii City-raion
is divided into 100 pre-
cincts, common to all
elections

Oktiabr'skii City-raion is divided into
250 districts for elections to the
Oktiabr'skii City-raion Soviet

This chart is based on information in "Shiritsia razmakh predvybornoi raboty," **VL** (Jan. 28, 1963), p. 1.

Administrative-Territorial Structure of Leningrad, Oblast and City, 1963

RSFSR

Leningrad Oblast

Leningrad Oblast
Industrial Soviet

12 cities

13 cities and
40 settlements

Leningrad Oblast
Agricultural Soviet

10 agricultural raions

314 villages

p settlement (poselok)

c city

City Soviet of Greater Leningrad

City-raions

VASILEOSTROVSKII

VYBORGSKII

Pargolovo p

Levashovo p

DZERZHINSKII

ZHDANOVSKII

KALININSKII

KIROVSKII

KUIBYSHEVSKII

LENINSKII

MOSKOVSKII

NEVSKII

OKTIABR'SKII

PETROGRADSKII

SMOL'NINSKII

FRUNZENSKII

Suburban raions

KOLPINSKII

Pontonnyi p

Ust'-izhora p

Petro-Slavianka p

KRONSHTADTSKII

PETRODVORSOVYI

Strel'na p

PUSHKINSKII

Pavlovsk c

Alexandrovskaia p

Shushary p

Tiarlevo p

SESTRORETSKII

Zelenogorsk c

Repino p

Komarovo p

Ushkovo p

Lisii Nos p

Pesochnyi p

94

APPENDIX D

Notes

Appendix D shows the administrative-territorial structure of Leningrad at the time of the 1963 elections using the same schematic representation as Appendix A. Newspaper accounts (the basis for Appendix E) list 12 settlements within Greater Leningrad, whereas SSSR. Administrativno-terriotrial'noe delenie Soiuznykh Respublik lists 14, as shown here; this latter work also indicates that Sestroretskii suburban raion was made a city-raion after the elections. Another apparent change concerns Vyborgskii city-raion, which was formerly Stalinskii.

Sources

SSSR. Administrativno-territorial'noe delenie Soiuznykh Respublik, na 1 aprelia 1963 g. (Moskva: Izd-vo "Izvestiia," 1963), pp. 113-15.

"Administrativno-territorial'noe delenie Leningrada i prigorodov," Biulleten' Ispolkoma Leningradskogo Gorodskogo Soveta (no. 1, Jan., 1962), pp. 15-16; and "O rassirenii gorodskoi cherty Leningrada," (no. 2, Jan., 1963), pp. 1-2.

"Itogi vyborov...," LP (Mar. 6, 1963), p. 1.

"V Sovety izbrany...," Smena (Mar. 20, 1963), p. 3.

APPENDIX E

Quantitative Data on the 1963 Elections

Level	Number of deputies	Population represented (end of 1961)
RSFSR		
Supreme Soviet	874	122,084,000
Republic plus local soviets	1,036,000	122,084,000
Party members	44.9%	...
Women	41.9%	...
Elected for the first time	59.1%	...
Leningrad Oblast		
From Leningrad Oblast to RSFSR Soviet	11	1,295,000
Leningrad Oblast Industrial Soviet	106	713,000
All subordinate soviets	4,831	713,000
Leningrad Oblast Agricultural Soviet	100	582,000
All subordinate soviets	9,604	582,000
Greater Leningrad		
From Greater Leningrad to RSFSR Soviet	23	3,498,000
Greater Leningrad City Soviet	595	3,498,000
All subordinate soviets	5,128	3,498,000

Sources

Narodnoe khoziaistvo SSR v 1961 godu (Moskva: Gosstatizdat, 1962), pp. 9, 16, 20.

"Pobeda narodnogo bloka," LP (Mar. 6, 1963), p. 1.

"V Sovety izbrany...," Smena (Mar. 20, 1963), p. 3.

"Izbiratel'nye okruga po vyboram v Verkhovnyi Sovet RSFSR," VL (Jan. 12, 1963), p. 1.

Calendar of Events

Days Before Election	1963 Date	Statute Article PR	PM	Activity	Responsible Organ
45	17 Jan.	26	50	Lists of districts published	Presidium of RSFSR Supreme Soviet; Exec. Committees of city and city-raion soviets
40	22 Jan.	37		Central Election Commission of RSFSR formed	Presidium of Supreme Soviet, RSFSR
40	22 Jan.		50	List of districts published for local elections	Executive Committees of city and city-raion soviets
40	22 Jan.		52	City election commissions formed	Presidium of Supreme Soviet, RSFSR
40	22 Jan.		52	City-raion election commissions formed	Executive Committee of city soviet
	25 Jan.			Manufacture signs for hqs. of district election commissions	Theatrical-Artistic Production Kombinat, on order of city-raion Executive Committees
35	26 Jan.	41		RSFSR election districts formed	Executive Committee, Leningrad City Soviet
35	26 Jan.		55	District election commissions formed for city and city-raions	Executive Committees of city and city-raions
30	31 Jan.	28	66	Election precincts formed	Executive Committees of city-raion soviets
	5 Feb.			Precinct election commissions supplied with telephones	City Telephone Board, on orders of city-raion soviets

Appendix F (continued)

Days Before Election	1963 Date	Statute Article PR	PM	Activity	Responsible Organ
25	6 Feb.	45	75	Precinct election commissions formed	Executive Committees of city-raion soviets
20	11 Feb.	64		Voters informed daily of day and place of voting for RSFSR elections	Precinct election commissions
20	11 Feb.	53		Registration ends for RSFSR candidates	Nominating organizations, district commissions
20	11 Feb.	19	19	Lists of voters displayed for public inspection	Executive Committee of appropriate soviet
15	16 Feb.		93	Voters informed daily of day and place of voting for local elections	Precinct election commissions
15	16 Feb.		82	Registration ends for local candidates	Nominating organizations, district commissions
15	16 Feb.	57		Data on RSFSR candidates published	District election commissions
14	17 Feb.			Election day announced for People's Judges	Leningrad City Soviet
12	19 Feb.			Precincts formed for election of People's Judges	Precinct election commissions
10	21 Feb.			Lists of voters for People's Judges displayed	Executive Committees of corresponding soviets
10	21 Feb.		86	Data on local candidates published	District election commissions

Days Before Election	1963 Date	Statute Article PR	PM	Activity	Responsible Organ
10	21 Feb.	59	88	Ballots sent to precinct election commissions	District election commissions
7	24 Feb.			Candidates for People's Judges registered	Executive Committee of Leningrad City Soviet
5	26 Feb.			Data on candidates for People's Judges published	Executive Committee of Leningrad City Soviet
	25 Feb.			Polling places prepared	(not stated)
5				Plan for keeping a running account of balloting	Party organs

Note

The deadline stated by the newspapers and the Executive Committees of the Leningrad and Moscow City Soviets are two days in advance of the date required by election statutes, counting the day before elections as the first day. Where there is conflict, the date established by the statute has been given.

Sources
(in addition to the election statutes)

Polozhenie o vyborakh raionnykh (gorodskikh) narodnykh sudov RSFSR (Moskva: Gosiurizdat, 1960), 31 pp.

O podgotovke i provedenii vyborov v Moskovskii gorodskoi, raionnye, gorodskie, sel'skie i poselkovye Sovety deputatov trudiashchikhsia gor. Moskvy i lesoparkovogo zashchitnogo poiasa, " Biulleten' Ispokoma Moskovskogo Gorodskogo Soveta (no. 2, 1961), p. 28.

Khorosho podgotovit'sia k vyboram v Sovety, " VL (Jan. 14, 1963), p. 1.

V Ispolkome Lensoveta. O podgotovke k vyboram v Verkhovnyi Sovet RSFSR i mestnye Sovety, " LP (Jan. 15, 1963), p. 1.

Norms of Representation

PM Art.	Level of Soviet	No. of Election Districts	Residents per District
(PR 25)	RSFSR Supreme Soviet	874	150,000
25	Krai and oblast	100 or more	7,000
25	Autonomous oblast	100 or more	2,000
33	National okrug	75 or more	1,500
41	Raion	75 or more	1,000
49	Moscow and Leningrad	no set norm	6,000
	Cities over 500,000	500 or less	1,100
	300,000 - 500,000	450 or less	850
	100,000 - 300,000	350 or less	400
	15,000 - 100,000	250 or less	300
	under 15,000	50 or less	300
49	City-raion of city over 25,000 population	250 or less	500
49	City-raion of city under 25,000	50	
57	Villages and settlements over 2,500	75 or less	100
	500 - 2,500	25	
	under 500	less than 25	

NOTE: According to the statutes (PR, art. 25; PM art. 10), one deputy is
elected from each district.

APPENDIX H

Membership on Election Commissions
of Greater Leningrad

PM Art.	Type of commission	Number of commissions	Members on each	Total members
	Administrative-territorial unit	34	...	258
52	Leningrad City Electoral Commission	1	9-12	9
52	City and suburban raions	19	9-12	171
52	Cities subordinate to Leningrad	2	9-12	18
60	Settlements subordinate to Leningrad	12	5-7	60
	District (one per deputy)	5,746	...	28,084
(PR 41)	RSFSR districts	23	11	253
55	Leningrad City Soviet districts	595	5-7	2,975
55	City and suburban raion districts	4,227	5-7	21,135
63	Districts of settlements subordinate to Leningrad	784	4	3,136
55	Districts of cities subordinate to Leningrad	117	5-7	585
75	Precinct	1,637	7-11	11,459
	Totals	7,418		39,801

Notes

Information is based on election statutes and data supplied by the Executive Committee of the Leningrad City Soviet. The total number of members is arrived at by multiplying the number of commissions by the fewest members prescribed for each commission.

In "Khorosho podgotovit'sia k vyboram v Sovety, " VL (Jan. 14, 1963), a total of 6,216 "election commissions" is given for Leningrad instead of the 7,418 calculated here. The article does not, however, specify the type of commission and whether or not the figure applies to Greater Leningrad.

Sources
(in addition to PR and PM)

"V Leningradskoi gorodskoi izbiratel'noi komissii, " VL (Jan. 29, 1963), p. 1.

"V Sovety izbrany... , " Smena (Mar. 20, 1963), p. 3.

APPENDIX I

Form for Report of a District Election Commission on the Nomination of a Candidate

Протокол Окружной
избирательной комиссии о регистрации кандидатов в депутаты

_____
наименование избираемого Совета

Совета депутатов трудящихся

_____ района, _____ края, области РСФСР

(составляется отдельно на каждого кандидата)

_____ _____ —196__ года
число   месяц составления протокола

_____ избирательный округ № _____
наименование избирательного округа

Настоящий протокол составлен _____ Окружной

избирательной комиссией по выборам в ____ _____ Совет
наименование избираемого Совета

депутатов трудящихся, состоящей из нижеперечисленных представителей общественных организаций и обществ трудя-

щихся и утвержденной решением исполнительного комитета _____
наименование исполнительного комитета Совета, утвердившего состав

_____ Совета депутатов трудящихся от _____ дня _____ месяца 196____года:
избирательной комиссии

Председатель	_____ от _____	
Заместитель председателя	фамилия, имя, отчество ___ от _____	от какой общественной организации или общества трудящихся
Секретарь	_____ от _____	
Члены:	_____ от _____	
	_____ от _____	
	_____ от _____	
	_____ от _____	
	_____ от _____	

Рассмотрев поступившие в Окружную избирательную комиссию протоколы

общественных организаций, обществ трудящихся и общих собраний о выставлении кандидатом

в депутаты _____ Совета
наименование избираемого Совета

депутатов трудящихся по _____ избирательному округу № _____
наименование избирательного округа

_____
фамилия, имя, отчество

и заявление о его согласии баллотироваться по данному избирательному округу от выставивших организаций,

Окружная избирательная комиссия, на основании представленных документов, установила,

что _____
фамилия, имя, отчество

выставлен кандидатом в депутаты в полном соответствии с „Положением о выборах в краевые, областные, окруж-

ные, районные, городские, сельские и поселковые Советы депутатов трудящихся РСФСР".

Appendix I (continued)

На основании „Положения о выборах", Окружная избирательная комиссия постановила: зарегистрировать

кандидатом в депутаты ———————————————————————————— Совета

наименование избираемого Совета

депутатов трудящихся ————————————————————————————

фамилия, имя и отчество,

——

год рождения, место жительства,

——

партийность, занятие

для баллотировки по ———————————————————————————— избирательному

наименование избирательного округа

округу № ———— по выборам в ———————————————————————— Совет

наименование избираемого Совета

депутатов трудящихся, выставленного от ————————————————————————

наименование общественных организаций, обществ трудящихся и общих собраний,

——

выставивших кандидата в депутаты

На основании „Положения о выборах", включить кандидата в депутаты ——————————

фамилия,

————————————————————————— в избирательный бюллетень для баллотировки

имя и отчество

по ——————————————————————————— избирательному округу № ———————— по

наименование избирательного округа

выборам в ————————————————————————— Совет депутатов трудящихся.

наименование избираемого Совета

Настоящее постановление опубликовать для всеобщего сведения.

При регистрации кандидата в депутаты присутствовали представители общественных организаций и обществ трудящихся, а также представители печати:

————————————————————— от ————————————————————————

фамилия, имя и отчество — от какой общественной организации, общества трудящихся, газеты, журнала

————————————————————— от ————————————————————————

————————————————————— от ————————————————————————

————————————————————— от ————————————————————————

Настоящий протокол регистрации составлен в двух экземплярах.

Один экземпляр протокола в запечатанном виде с нарочным посылается в соответствующую Краевую, Областную, Окружную, Районную, Городскую, Районную в городах, Сельскую или Поселковую избирательную комиссию.

Другой экземпляр протокола передается на хранение исполнительному комитету соответствующего краевого или областного, окружного, районного, городского, районного в городах, сельского, поселкового Совета депутатов трудящихся.

Председатель Окружной   **Зам. председателя Окружной**
избирательной комиссии   **избирательной комиссии**

М. П.

Члены Окружной   **Секретарь Окружной**
избирательной комиссии   **избирательной комиссии**

APPENDIX J

Candidate's Letter of Agreement to Run

To: District Election Commission
        for elections to the Smol'ninskii
        City-<u>raion</u> Soviet of Toilers' Deputies

From: Petrova, Aleksandra Nikolaevna
        born 1924
        residing at: Leningrad, Nevskii Prospekt, house 4/7, apt. 2

AGREEMENT

I express my deep gratitude to the collective of toilers which
nominated me a candidate to the Smol'ninskii Raisovet of Toilers'
Deputies; I agree to run for the post of deputy in election district
47. I will make every effort to justify the faith of the voters.

February 6, 1963   Petrova

APPENDIX K

Sample of a Local Election Ballot

ИЗБИРАТЕЛЬНЫЙ БЮЛЛЕТЕНЬ

„———" —————— 196 —— года

Оставьте в избирательном бюллетене фамилию ОДНОГО кандидата, за которого Вы голосуете, остальных вычеркните.

Фамилия, имя, отчество кандидата в депутаты	Кем выставлен кандидатом в депутаты

Председатель ————— Окружной избирательной

This sample ballot for USSR elections is reproduced from "Polozhenie o vyborakh v Verkhovnyi Sovet SSSR," (Moskva: Izdatel'stvo "Izvestiia," 1962), p. 48.

NOTES

Abbreviations

VL--Vechernii Leningrad, daily (evening) paper.

LP--Leningradskaia Pravda, daily (morning) paper.

PM--Polozhenie o vyborakh v kraevye, oblastnye, okruzhnye, raionnye, gorodskie, sel'skie i poselkovye Sovety deputatov trudiashchikhsia RSFSR. The local election statute of the RSFSR. References are to article numbers.

PR-- Polozhenie o vyborakh v Verkhovnyi Sovet RSFSR. The republic election statute for the RSFSR. References are to article numbers.

Introduction

1. George Barr Carson, Jr., Electoral Practices in the U.S.S.R. (New York: Frederick A. Praeger, 1955). Howard R. Swearer, "Popular Participation: Myths and Realities, " Problems of Communism, IX (Sept. -Oct. 1960), pp. 42-51; and "The Functions of Soviet Local Elections, " Midwest Journal of Political Science, V (May, 1961), pp. 129-49.

Some of the standard works are: Merle Fainsod, How Russia Is Ruled (Cambridge: Harvard University Press, rev. ed., 1963), pp. 381-83. John N. Hazard, The Soviet System of Government (Chicago: Chicago University Press, 3rd ed., 1963), pp. 50-55. Herbert McClosky and John E. Turner, The Soviet Dictatorship (New York: McGraw-Hill Book Company, Inc., 1960), pp. 324-32.

2. "Itogi vyborov v mestnye Sovety deputatov trudiashchikhsia, " Leningradskaia Pravda (Mar. 8, 1963), p. 1. Newspaper hereafter abbreviated as LP.

3. "Moguchee edinstvo, " LP (Mar. 19, 1963), p. 1.

4. See, e.g., "Ob uluchshenii deiatel'nosti Sovetov deputatov trudiashchikhsia i ikh sviazei s massami, " in KPSS o rabote Sovetov (Moskva: Gosiurizdat, 1959), p. 474. This important document on the soviets was a decision of the Central Committee of the CPSU, dated January 22, 1957.

Chapter 1

1. Some important sources for the 1962-63 changes are: N.S. Khrushchev, "Perestroit' partiinye organy v sootvetstvii s zadachami kommunisticheskogo stroitel'stva, " Razvitie ekonomiki SSSR i partiinoe rukovodstvo narodnym khoziaistvom (Moskva: Gospolitizdat, 1962), pp. 15-28; also printed in LP (Nov. 20, 1962). The action of the Central Committee is based on Khrushchev's suggestion, O razvitii ekonomiki SSSR i perestroike partiinogo rukovodstva narodnym khoziaistvom, Postanovlenie Plenuma TsK KPSS po dokladu tovarishcha N.S. Khrushcheva, priniatoe 23 noiabria 1962 goda (Moskva: Gospolitizdat, 1962)see also "Ob izmeneniiakh v administrativno-territorial'nom delenii, "

Vedomosti Verkhovnogo Soveta SSSR (no. 12, Mar. 20, 1963), pp. 207-83, and "Reorganizatsiia kraevykh, oblastnykh i raionnykh Sovetov deputatov trudiashchikhsia, " Biulleten' Ispolkoma Lengor-soveta (no. 4, 1963), p. 9. The execution of this reorganization is in itself an interesting case study in the way administrative changes begin with a suggestion at the center and spread to the periphery. The structure for the USSR at the time of the elections dealt with here can be found in SSSR. Administrativno-territorial'noe delenie soiuznykh respublik, Na 1 aprelia 1963 goda. (Moskva: Izd-vo Izvestiia Sovetov deputatov trudiashchikhsia SSSR, Izd 12-e, 1963); see especially the material on Leningrad city and oblast, pp. 111-15.

Some of the more important sources on the abandonment of the dual system are: "Postanovlenie Plenuma TsKKPSS ob ob''e-dinenii promyshlennykh i sel'skikh oblastnykh, kraevykh partiinykh organizatsii, " Pravda (Nov. 17, 1964), p. 1; a terse phrase from this party directive initiated the action to restore single soviet bodies. "Vernost' Leninskim organizatsionnym printsipam, " Pravda (Nov. 18, 1964), p. 1; translated in: Current Digest of the Soviet Press, XVI (Dec. 2, 1964), pp. 3, 4, 16. "V Rossiiskoi Federatsii--1.551 raion, " Pravda (Jan. 14, 1965), p. 2; translated in: Current Digest of the Soviet Press, XVII (Feb. 3, 1965), p. 31. Vedomosti Verkhovnogo Soveta RSFSR (no. 3, Jan. 18, 1965), art. 12-82, pp. 25-73; see esp. art. 47, pp. 46-47, for Leningrad oblast. "Ob izmeneniiakh v administrativno-territorial'nom delenii, " Vedo-mosti Verkhovnogo Soveta SSSR (no. 8, 1965), pp. 107-60. Shelest, P. "Raionnoe zveno, " Pravda (Feb. 6, 1965), p. 2; translated in: Current

Digest of the Soviet Press, XVII (Mar. 3, 1965), pp. 19-21. Azovkin, I. A. "Mestnye Sovety deputatov trudiashchikhsia na sovremennom etape kommunisticheskogo stroitel'stva, " Sovetskoe gosudarstvo i pravo (no. 3, Mar., 1965), pp. 3-13. Kochubei, A. "Vsemi silami ukrepit' raionnoe zveno, " Sovety deputatov trudiashchikhsia (no. 3, Mar., 1965), pp. 26-30. SSSR, Administrativno-territorial'noe delenie soiuznykh respublik, Ianvar' 1965 god (Moscow: Izd-vo "Izvestiia, " 1965); presents the new structure for the entire USSR.

2. Narodnoe khoziaistvo SSSR v 1961 godu. Statisticheskii ezhegodnik (Moskva: Tsentral'noe statisticheskoe upravlenie pri Sovete Ministrov SSSR, 1962), p. 36.

3. Polozhenie o vyborakh v kraevye, oblastnye, okruzhnye, raionnye, gorodskie, sel'skie i poselkovye Sovety deputatov trudiashchikhsia RSFSR (Moskva: Gosiurizdat, 1963), ch. IV. The title of this statute for local elections will hereafter be abbreviated to PM. See also Appendix G for information on the national okrug.

4. Exact information as to which village or workers' settlement has a soviet is difficult to obtain. Decisions on the matter are made by the executive committee of the next higher soviet, and as a rule this information is not made public. In fact, only a limited quantity of information on the proceedings of executive committees is published, and then only by those few bodies which issue Bulletins.

5. Since 1957, cities have been divided into four categories, those of krai, oblast, raion and republic subordination. For the RSFSR this is set forth in the edict of the Supreme Soviet, "O

poriadke otneseniia naselennykh punktov k kategorii gorodov, rabochikh i kurortnykh poselkov, " Vedomosti Verkhovnogo Soveta RSFSR (no. 1, st. 3, 1957), pp. 18-19. Professor Lepeshkin lists only three categories, treating as one single category the krai and oblast'; see A.I. Lepeshkin et al., Kurs Sovetskogo gosudarstvennogo prava (Moskva: Gosiurizdat, 1962), II, 235. For other discussions see: D. L. Zlatopol'skii, Gosudarstvennoe ustroistvo SSSR (Moskva: Gosiurizdat, 1960), p. 286; and R.S. Pavlovskii and M.A. Shafir, Administrativno-territorial'noe ustroistvo SSSR (Moskva: Gosiurizdat, 1961), pp. 88-91. Leningrad and Moscow are classified as cities of republic subordination in Konstitutsiia (osnovnoi zakon) Rossiiskoi Sovetskoi Federativnoi Sotsialisticheskoi Respubliki (Moskva: Gosiurizdat, 1962), art. 101.

6. See the annotation to art. 78 of the election statute for the USSR: Polozhenie o vyborakh v Verkhovnyi Sovet SSSR. S prilozheniem form dokumentov, ustanovlennykh prezidiumom Verkhovnogo Soveta SSSR i Tsentral'noi Izbiratel'noi Komissiei, i poiasneniiami (Moskva: Izdatel'stvo "Izvestiia, " 1962), p. 31.

7. "Ukaz Prezidiuma Verkhovnogo Soveta RSFSR o provedenii vyborov v Verkhovnyi Sovet RSFSR i v kraevye, oblastnye, okruzhnye, raionnye, gorodskie, sel'skie i poselkovye Sovety deputatov trudiashchikhsia RSFSR, " Verchernii Leningrad (Jan. 7, 1963), p. 1. Newspaper hereafter abbreviated to VL. The above edict is also found in Vedomosti Verkhovnogo Soveta RSFSR (no. 1, st. 1, Jan. 10, 1963), p. 5.

8. PM, art. 50; Polozhenie o vyborakh v Verkhovnyi Sovet

RSFSR (Moskva: Gosiurizdat, 1963), art. 26. The title of the latter statute, for republic elections, hereafter abbreivated to PR.

9. "Izbirtael'nye okruga po vyboram v Verkhovnyi Sovet RSFSR, " VL (Jan. 12, 1963), p. 1.

10. "V Leningradskoi gorodskoi izbiratel'noi komissii, " VL (Jan. 29, 1963), p. 1; and "V Sovety izbrany. . . , " Smena (Mar. 20, 1963), p. 3.

11. See, e. g. , "Tipovoe polozhenie o zhilishchnoi kontore zhilishchnogo upravleniia ispolkoma raisoveta, " Biulleten' Ispol-koma Lengorsoveta (no. 5, 1960), pp. 12-14. The statute for the housing office does not specifically assign to the head of the office the function of assisting the city in administrative matters, for his duties are principally to rent and care for the property under his control with the assistance of a secretarial staff and a group of repairmen. However, he does rent the apartments and it is his record of inhabitants which allows him to furnish the necessary information to the election authorities.

12. "V Ispolkome Lensoveta. O podgotovke k vyboram v Verkhovnyi Sovet RSFSR i mestnye Sovety, " LP (Jan. 15, 1963), p. 1. This article mentions the deadline for forming precincts "obshchie po vyboram v Verkhovnyi Sovet RSFSR i mestnye Sovety. . . "

13. "V Leningradskoi gorodskoi izbiratel'noi komissii, " VL (Jan. 29, 1963), p. 1; and "Khorosho podgotovit'sia k vyboram v Sovety, " VL (Jan. 14, 1963), p. 1.

14. "Navstrechu vyboram," VL (Jan. 11, 1963), p. 1.

15. PR, art. 38.

16. "Vydvizhenie kandidatov v sostav Tsentral'noi izbiratel'noi komissii po vyboram v Verkhovnyi Sovet RSFSR," VL (Jan. 14, 1963), p. 1.

17. PM, art. 56; see also Appendices I and J for registration documents.

18. PR, art. 42.

19. "Spravochnye materialy o mestnykh Sovetakh deputatov trudiashchikhsia, izbrannykh v marte 1961 goda," Sovety deputatov trudiashchikhsia (no. 2, Feb., 1963), pp. 94-95.

20. PM, art. 76; PR, art. 46.

Chapter 2

1. Swearer, "The Functions of Soviet Local Elections."

2. See Appendix F for a calendar of election activities.

3. PM, art. 77, 78; PR, art. 49, 50.

4. The new law on recall is Zakon Rossiiskoi Sovetskoi Federativnoi Sotsialisticheskoi Respubliki o poriadke otzyva deputata kraevogo, oblastnogo, okruzhnogo, raionnogo, gorodskogo, sel'skogo, poselkovogo Soveta deputatov trudiashchikhsia RSFSR. Priniat na III sessii Verkhovnogo Soveta RSFSR piatogo sozyva (Moskva: Gosiurizdat, 1961), 7 pp. This is modelled on "Zakon o

poriadke otzyva deputata Verkhovnogo Soveta SSSR. Priniat tret'ei sessiei Verkhovnogo Soveta SSSR, 30 oktiabria 1959 goda, " in Spravochnik partiinogo rabotnika (Moskva: Gospolitizdat, vypusk tretii, 1961), pp. 588-89.

5. The quotation is from "The Destruction of Parliamentarism, " part 3 of State and Revolution, and runs in part: "The way out of parliamentarism, naturally, is not the destruction of representative institutions and electoral practices [vybornost'], but rather the transformation of representative institutions from talking shops [govoril'ni] into 'working' institutions... Look at any parliamentary country... In the parliaments they just chatter, for the express purpose of making fools of the 'simple folk'. " V. I. Lenin, Sochineniia (2nd and 3rd eds.), IX, 162. This is not an isolated remark by Lenin, as a perusal of his works will show. He accused the Russian Duma of "parliamentarism" and "parliamentary cretinism" for debating about their views on truth. What Lenin wanted was a body of representatives which would educate and lead the proletariat; he wanted action, not words. See also: IX, 162; X, 131; XV, 555-56; and XVII, 310-11.

6. "Otkrytoe pis'mo izbiratel'nym komissiiam po vyboram v Verkhovnye Sovety soiuznykh respublik, " LP (Feb. 5, 1963), p. 1. Any list of candidates reveals this; see e. g. "Spisok kandidatov v deputaty Leningradskogo gorodskogo Soveta deputatov trudiash-chikhsia, zaregistrirovannykh okruzhnymi izbiratel'nymi komissiiami, " VL (Feb. 19, 1963), pp. 2-6.

7. For a substantiation of this view, see T. H. Rigby,

"Soviet Local Government and Democracy, " The Australian Outlook, 8 (Mar. 1954), pp. 19-31.

8. PM, art. 81; PR, art. 53.

9. "Kollektiv Kirovskogo zavoda vydvinul kandidatami v deputaty Verkhovnogo Soveta RSFSR Nikitu Sergeevicha Khrushcheva, Ivana Davydovicha Leonova, " VL (Jan. 29, 1963), p. 1.

10. "Rech' tovarishcha F. R. Kozlova, " VL (Feb. 27, 1963), p. 1.

11. "Rech' tovarishcha N. S. Khrushcheva, " VL (Feb. 28, 1963), pp. 1-2; also published as N. S. Khrushchev, Rech' na sobranii izbiratelei Kalininskogo izbiratel'nogo okruga goroda Moskvy, 27 fevralia 1963 goda (Moskva: Gospolitizdat, 1963).

12. PR, art. 53.

13. "Spisok kandidatov..., " VL (Feb. 19, 1963); although registration was said to have been completed, only 585 of the total 595 candidates were listed at this time.

14. PM, art. 82.

15. "V gorodskoi izbiratel'noi komissii, " VL (Feb. 16, 1963), p. 1.

16. PM, art. 83; PR, art. 54.

17. PM, art. 84; PR, art. 55; see also Appendix I for a facsimile of a district commission report.

18. L. Bus'ko, "Navstrechu vyboram v Sovety. Deputatskaia estafeta, " VL (Feb. 1, 1963), p. 2. This is an article on

the training of deputies by the head of the Organization-Instruction Department of the Leningrad City Soviet.

19. PM, art. 86; PR, art. 57.

20. "Spisok kandidatov...," VL (Feb. 19, 1936); and "Navstrechu vyboram v Sovety: Registratsiia kandidatov v deputaty Verkhovnogo Soveta RSFSR," VL (Feb. 12, 1963), p. 1.

21. PM, art. 19; PR, art. 19.

22. For information on People's Judges, see: Konstitutsiia ...SSSR..., art. 109; Konstitutsiia...RSFSR..., art. 113; Polozhenie o vyborakh raionnykh (gorodskikh) narodnykh sudov RSFSR (Moskva: Gosiurizdat, 1960), art. 14 and 16, in which the special position of the Executive Committee of the Leningrad City Soviet is set forth in regard to the election of People's Judges; and Nauchno-prakticheskii kommentarii k zakonu o sudoustroistve RSFSR (Moskva: Gosiurizdat, 1962), pp. 68-80. The lay assessors (narodnye zasedateli) are not elected by the voters at large, but are chosen in meetings at places of work; cf. art. 1 of the Polozhenie cited here, and "Vybory narodnykh zasedatelei v raionnye narodnye sudy Leningrada," Biulleten' Ispolkoma Lengorsoveta (no. 5, 1963), p. 17.

23. "Vybory narodnykh sudei raionnykh narodnykh sudov g. Leningrada," VL (Feb. 25, 1963), p. 1.

24. Polozhenie o vyborakh...narodnykh sudov RSFSR, art. 69; see also the calendar of events in Appendix F.

25. "Soobshchenie ob itogakh vyborov narodnykh sudei raionnykh narodnykh sudov," VL (Mar. 7, 1963), p. 1.

Chapter 3

1. PM, art. 93.

2. See for example the "Nashi kandidaty" series beginning on February 7 in Vechernii Leningrad.

3. PM, art. 88; PR, art. 59.

4. This is the interpretation offered by one citizen of Leningrad.

5. "Nashi kandidaty v deputaty: Sluzhenie liudiam, Odin den' Anny Vasil'evoi, Spravedlivyi chelovek, " VL (Mar. 1, 1963), p. 1; "Bez ostanovki proizvodstva, " and "Nash deputat, " pictures in LP (Feb. 22, 1963), p. 2.

6. L. Plyshevskaia, "Nashi kandidaty v deputaty: Budni, dostoinye slavy, " VL (Feb. 12, 1963), p. 2.

7. The New Soviet Society [text of the Program of the Communist Party of the Soviet Union], with annotations and an introduction by Herbert Ritvo (New York: The New Leader, 1962), pp. 55-70. "Krizis mirovogo kapitalizma, " Programma Kommunisticheskoi Partii Sovetskogo Soiuza (Moskva: Gospolitizdat, 1961), pp. 25-35.

8. N.S. Khrushchev, "O programme Kommunisticheskoi Partii Sovetskogo Soiuza, " XXII S'ezd Kommunisticheskoi Partii Sovetskogo Soiuza, stenograficheskii otchet (Moskva: Gospolitizdat, 1962), I, 148-257; see especially the comments on p. 215.

9. Khrushchev, Rech' na sobranii..., pp. 4-7; these

four pages at the beginning of the speech are a derisive account of American parties, elections, and politics in general.

10. See, e.g., I. Galkin, "Dolg Sovetskikh uchenykh, " Mezhdunarodnaia Zhizn' (no. 2, 1957), pp. 129-31.

11. A.I. Lepeshkin et al., Kurs Sovetskogo gosudarstven- nogo prava (Moskva: Gosiurizdat, 1962); see especially II, 572-86 for his treatment of the bourgeois electoral systems.

12. Mikhail Anatol'evich Krutogolov, Antidemokraticheskaia sushchnost' burzhuaznykh vyborov (Moskva: Gosiurizdat, 1963); this author is apparently a specialist in popular propaganda and western elections; see also his Vybory u nas i u nikh (Moskva: Izd-vo IMO, 1962) and Vybory v SSSR i v burzhuaznykh stranakh (Moskva: Izdatel'stvo Instituta Mezhdunarodnykh Otnoshenii, 1959).

13. "SShA, " Izbiratel'nye sistemy stran mira (Moskva: Gospolitizdat, 1961), pp. 180-90.

14. "Bol'shaia lozh' burzhuaznogo mira, " Sputnik izbira- telia (Moskva: Gospolitizdat, 1962), pp. 189-253.

15. "Svobodnyi mir bez svobod, " VL (Feb. 27, 1963), p. 3; and M. Strepukhov, "Narod--khoziain strany, " VL (Mar. 1, 1963), p. 2.

16. "Vstrechi izbiratelei s kandidatami v deputaty, " VL (Feb. 16, 1963), p. 1.

17. See, e.g., "O rabote po vypolneniiu nakazov izbiratelei," Biulleten' Ispolkoma Lengorsoveta (no. 12, 1962), pp. 13-15.

18. "Navstrechu vyboram, " VL (Jan. 11, 1963), p. 1.

19. "V partiinykh organizatsiiakh. 10 tysiach agitatorov, " VL (Mar. 1, 1963), p. 2.

20. "Khorosho podgotovit'sia k vyboram v Sovety, " VL (Jan. 14, 1963), p. 1.

21. "V Sovety izbrany. . . , " Smena (Mar. 20, 1963), p. 3.

22. "Nash kommentarii. S zhivym slovom k izbirateliam, " VL (Jan. 28, 1963), p. 1.

23. "Navstrechu vyboram v Sovety. Dobro pozhalovat' v agitpunkt, " VL (Feb. 5, 1963), p. 1.

24. "Vechera voprosov i otvetov dlia izbiratelei, " VL (Feb. 28, 1963), p. 2; for a description of the new form of deputy group see Liudmila Semenovna Bus'ko, Deputatskie gruppy (Leningrad: Lenizdat, 1963), 53 pp.

25. "Shiritsia razmakh predvybornoi raboty, " VL (Jan. 28, 1963), p. 1.

26. "Nash kommentarii. . . , " VL (Jan. 28, 1963).

27. V. Rudyk and V. Georgiev, "Beseda dushevnaia, " VL (Feb. 12, 1963), p. 1.

28. PR, art. 38.

29. PM, art. 99; PR, art. 70.

30. "Nash kommentarii. . . , " VL (Jan. 28, 1963); the author says Shakespeare is being quoted by the American, Albert Kahn.

One wonders whether he is aware that Shakespeare has also been quoted by the Englishman, Aldous Huxley.

31. Viktor Fomich Kotok, Sovetskaia predstavitel'naia sistema (Moskva: Gosiurizdat, 1963), p. 37.

32. "O podgotovke i provedenii vyborov v Moskovskii gorodskoi, raionnye, gorodskie, sel'skie i poselkovye Sovety deputatov trudiashchikhsia gor. Moskvy i lesoparkovogo zashchitnogo poiasa, " Biulleten' Ispolkoma Moskovskogo gorodskogo Soveta (no. 2, 1961), pp. 25-29; this reference from Moscow election activities is also in the general calendar of Appendix F.

33. PM, art. 21, 102; PR, art. 21, 73.

34. "Pochetnoe zadanie. Izbiratel'nye uchastki v poezdakh, " VL (Feb. 5, 1963), p. 1; and "Izbiratel'nyi uchastok v poezde, " VL (Mar. 1, 1963), p. 1.

35. PM, art. 100; PR, art. 71.

Chapter 4

1. PM, art. 12; PR, art. 12.

2. PM, art. 95; PR, art. 45.

3. The activities of the deputy are a subject to be treated elsewhere; here it is necessary to note that he has no power in the Western sense of the word. Soviet statutes do not originate with the soviet, as ordinances do with an American city council. The Soviet deputy approves acts of his Executive Committee and its

subordinate boards, he does not formulate or alter them. He can bring only the most limited kind of pressure to bear on administrative organs in two ways.

One way is the right of inquiry into the activities of administrative offices. On this subject see: Dem'ian Nikolaevich Bakhrakh, Pravo zaprosa deputatov mestnykh Sovetov (Moskva: Gosiurizdat, 1960), 50 pp. This is a monograph based on research by a professional member of a local soviet.

The other way is to make "binding decisions" addressed to the units of an Executive Committee by Standing Commissions of the soviet. But this right is limited. In Moscow, for example, the Standing Commission can address a "binding decision" to the "heads of any organization in regard to all questions connected with the execution of decisions of the Moscow Soviet and its Executive Committee, with the exception of changes in the plan, budget, and distribution of material resources. " But the plan, budget, and material resources are the very heart of the matter. What this right amounts to, then, is simply the permission to remind heads of departments and boards that they are supposed to carry out the decisions of the Executive Committee. See "O postoiannykh kommissiakh Moskovskogo gorodskogo Soveta deputatov trudiashchikhsia, " Biulleten' Ispolkoma Mossoveta (no. 10, 1962), p. 9.

GLOSSARY OF RUSSIAN TERMS

Domovyi komitet (domkom)	House committee, a voluntary organization; an elected body of people who donate their time to organizational activities for the residents of one or a few apartment houses or other dwelling places
Doverennoe litso	"Sworn supporter" a person charged with agitating for a given candidate
Gorodskoi komitet (gorkom)	City party committee
Ispolnitel'nyi komitet (ispolkom)	Executive Committee, the permanently functioning body of a soviet at the local level
Krai	An administrative-territorial unit, comparable to an oblast.
Leningradskaia Promysh-lennaia Oblast	Leningrad Industrial Oblast
Leningradskaia Sel'skaia Oblast	Leningrad Agricultural Oblast
Oblast	The basic administrative-territorial unit beneath the level of the constituent republic; in size it corresponds to an American county or state

Obshchestvennaia organizatsiia	Public organization, a body with a fixed membership, e. g., the party, unions, cooperatives
Okrug	An election district, territory represented by one deputy; national okrug, an administrative-territorial unit
Partiinyi komitet (partkom)	Party committee, of an organization, institution, or enterprise
Polozhenie	Statute, when used as a term in electoral and administrative law
Poselok	Settlement, one of the smallest administrative-territorial units
Raionnyi komitet (raikom)	Raion party committee, city-raion party committee
Samodeiatel'naia organizatsiia	Voluntary organization, a body without a fixed membership, one purpose of which is to assist a soviet; some of them are: house committee (domovyi komitet), parents' committee (roditel'skii komitet), women's council (zhenskii sovet), street committee (ulichnyi komitet)
Selo	Village
Sovet narodnogo khoziaistva (Sovnarkhoz)	Council of the national economy, the directive body of one of the economic administrative regions.
Spisok izbiratelei	List of voters

Uchastok	Precinct, also the polling place of a precinct
Udostoverenie na pravo golosovaniia	Absentee voter's certificate
Upravlenie	Board
Zhilishchnaia kontora (zhilkontora)	Housing office, an administrative and maintenance staff responsible for a number of living quarters
Zhilishchnoe upravlenie	Housing board, an organ of an Executive Committee in charge of housing matters